Development

and

Patronage

Selected articles from *Development in Practice*

Introduced by Melakou Tegegn

A Development in Practice Reader

Series Editor: Deborah Eade

Oxfam (UK and Ireland)   1997

Published by Oxfam (UK and Ireland)
First published 1997

© Oxfam (UK and Ireland) 1997

A catalogue record for this publication is available from the British Library.

ISBN 0 85598 376 0

Published by Oxfam (UK and Ireland), 274 Banbury Road, Oxford OX2 7DZ, UK
(registered as a charity, no. 202918)

Available from the following agents:
for Canada and the USA: Humanities Press International, 165 First Avenue, Atlantic Highlands, New Jersey NJ 07716-1289, USA; tel. (908) 872 1441; fax (908) 872 0717
for southern Africa: David Philip Publishers, PO Box 23408, Claremont, Cape Town 7735, South Africa; tel. (021) 644136; fax (021) 643358.

Available in Ireland from Oxfam in Ireland, 19 Clanwilliam Terrace, Dublin 2 (tel. 01 661 8544).

OX067/RB/97
Printed by Oxfam Print Unit

Oxfam (UK and Ireland) is a member of Oxfam International.

Contents

Preface

Deborah Eade

The nineteenth-century liberal historian, Lord Acton, famously observed that 'power tends to corrupt, and absolute power corrupts absolutely'. At the time this aphorism was coined, European imperial power was at its height and was assumed — by its rulers, merchants, and missionaries — to be both a natural right and a moral duty. In the words of Cecil Rhodes, the spearhead of British colonial interests in Southern Africa who died in 1902: 'I believe it to be my duty to God, my Queen and my Country to paint the whole map of Africa red, red from the Cape to Cairo. That is my creed, my dream and my mission.' History — and the liberation and anti-colonial movements that gained momentum after the 1939–1945 war — was to dash such dreams. However, they still haunt the world in the form of conflicts and structural problems that can be traced back to the cultural and political divisions imposed by imperialism.

And yet, in so many ways, the transfer of formal power has been a hollow victory for people in the South, where almost one quarter of the world's population survives in conditions of extreme poverty. With economic restructuring now proceeding apace at a global level, millions more are seeing their incomes and security collapse, while the United Nations Development Programme (UNDP) reports that the combined wealth of the world's seven richest men could eliminate poverty and provide access to basic social services for the poorest quarter of the world's population. It is a world which can deliver fizzy drinks and hamburgers to anyone who can afford to pay, and yet cannot guarantee enough to eat to millions more.

It is in this context that the Colombian anthropologist Arturo Escobar writes:

It is clear to most people that the post-World War II dream of development is dead. Asia, Africa, and Latin America are no closer to becoming developed than in 1945, when the powers of capital and technology were summoned to make them clones of the First World. The question is: what comes after development?[1]

The dream of development might well be dead: certainly, it is more like a nightmare for the millions of children who will die of avoidable causes — attributable to poverty — before the end of this century, as it is for the half-million poor women who die each year in child-birth. So wherein, then, lies the continuing power of this collective dream? Is the challenge to reclaim development and redirect it or — as the Mexican scholar and activist Gustavo Esteva heretically argues — to create alternatives to it?[2]

While the multilateral and regional development banks, and the major official donors, wield real power over the policies of governments and the welfare of ordinary people, the development dream is also conveyed more insidiously: ideologies, discourses, dogmas, myths, and metaphors can be so seductive and so all-encompassing that they come to be taken for granted.

Crude language such as 'the triumph of capitalism' or 'the defeat of communism' reveals the struggle for ideological as well as economic hegemony over the direction that development should take. That entire nations are classified as *developed* or *developing* or *least-developed* (but never *over-developed* and seldom *mal-developed*) further implies that development is a one-way street, and that progress can be hastened by a blend of (Bretton Woods-approved) policies, international co-operation, and diligence. The struggle then becomes a semantic one to 'name' development: 'sustainable' or 'exclusionary', 'market-led' or 'people-centred', 'gender-fair' or 'gender-blind', 'trickle-down' or 'bottom-up', concerned with basic needs or with basic rights. It is like blind-folded children pinning ever more awkward qualifying tails on to the donkey. Ditching the concept becomes impossible, since the development industry 'has a way of shaping the world and its "needs" in its own interests'.[3]

Influential Southern thinkers have stressed that, without removing our 'mind-forg'd mana-cles' and breaking out of all forms of patronage, we cannot conceive of the world in a liberated and liberating way.[4] This suggests that we should indeed forget about looking for 'paradigms' and focus our energies on other ways of exploring human potential. Yet these writers are also acutely aware that material and political inequality will not evaporate just by wishing away dependence or internalised sub-jugation, nor by being more benign in the exercise of power.

Nonetheless, development agencies, and particularly NGOs, do set themselves the task of building North–South 'partnerships' that claim to be based on solidarity and egali-tarianism, but are in fact mediated through the one-way transfer of resources. In trying to balance these competing (and not always compatible) agendas, it is fair to ask whether the aid-dominated nature of any such partnership makes it impossible to ask the big questions about development: most organisations (and individuals) find it painful to ask the big questions even of themselves! But, given that development agencies exist, and show no signs of being about to self-destruct, it is essential that they should seek constantly to improve the quality of their partnerships. That the whole mission of development may be misguided is not a reason for development agencies to adopt less than the highest achievable standards of integrity.

Most of the papers in this collection are written by experienced practitioners who have been in one way or another on both the receiving and the giving ends of the aid chain. They speak of the race to keep up with their funders' (or employers') changing fads — environment one year, gender the next; decentralisation today, impact-assessment tomorrow — and thus of the way in which financial dependence limits their scope for intellectual and political autonomy. They show how vested interests, whether in the pursuit of patriarchal power or just financial survival, introduce a gulf between rhetoric and practice; these are the hidden forces which ensure that power does not shift. They speak too of how an NGO with a distorted self-image will inevitably generate conflicts as it goes about its work; how an NGO can, by taking on more overtly political roles, thereby disempower and depoliticise the people's organisations that gave it some measure of representational authority in the first place; of participatory projects that can rely on participants' good behaviour only when a respected authority figure is present, and which are otherwise largely unresponsive to them; or agencies which impose on others their own world-view and ways of working, in the name of empowerment and partnership.

In various ways, contributors to this volume underline the importance of mutual transpar-ency, especially when financial dependence is a reality. This applies as much to the NGOs which depend on official sources of money as it does to the Southern recipients of their funds. Being clear about where power lies will not dispel inequality, but may allow for critical feedback and negotiation. At present, development agencies feel free to pick and choose their 'partners' and to change their agendas at will — and this fine. But then their language of 'partner-ship' and 'solidarity' is revealed as so much pious humbug.

'Transparency' calls for better insights into the powerful undercurrents that converge to pull an organisation off its intended course. We are all the products of the web of beliefs and social structures of which we are a part, and of the experiences that have marked us as individuals. There are, however, ways in which people can learn to understand and recognise the forces that drive them, and so be freer (not necessarily free!) to make choices about them. Development agencies perhaps need to undergo a similar therapeutic process every now and then. It is not enough to have a policy that commits them to, for example, gender equity and equality. Techniques and training can help. Affirmative-action policies can shift the centre of gravity. Steps can be taken to bring gender issues into the public arena. Battles can be fought. But the real changes need to happen at the most intimate level — within, as it were, the heart and mind of the organisation. The process of change is not easy. It takes time and often a lot of trouble.

An honest and transparent partnership also demands a high level of mutual accountability. To paraphrase the British Labour politician, Tony Benn, there are five key questions:

- Whom do you represent?
- Where do you get your money from?
- To whom are you formally accountable?
- To whom are you morally accountable?
- How can we get rid of you?

It is this last question that so resonates with what some of the Southern contributors in this volume have to say. How can local people get rid of NGOs and other external agencies whom they regard as intrusive or dangerous or who are obstructing communication between the relevant actors? Is there a real need for Northern NGOs to act as middle-men in channelling government aid to Southern NGOs? If so, whose needs are being served? And what does this imply about mutual accountability and trust, especially if the demands on Southern 'partners' are changing 'in part as a result of the demands for accountability from those who provide the NGOs with their funds and in part as a result of the growing resemblance of these NGOs to commercial organisations'.[5]

We end by returning to Lord Acton, who believed that liberty was 'the marrow of modern history'. A practising Catholic, he opposed the doctrine of papal infallibility. His argument was with dogma — the idea that truth comes always and only from one source — rather than with the pronouncements of the Pope as such. Similarly, as **Melakou Tegegn** argues in his introductory essay, the old development paradigm should be turned on its head. No one doubts that immense positive achievements have been made in the name of development. But that does not mean that the direction followed until now is the right, the best, or the only one. If it were, the gap between rich and poor would be shrinking, not growing. Nor is it a viable alternative to retreat into the micro-universe of local realities. Humanity needs to find new ways of communicating, of creating political spaces for marginalised people; what Tegegn calls working for 'globalisation from below'. This is too important to be left to development experts in Geneva, Washington, or London. Cross-cultural partnership is not just an option for the privileged few, nor simply a way of transferring resources from the North to the South. It is a political and moral necessity, a question of survival.

Notes

1 Arturo Escobar (1997), 'The United Nations and the end of development', reprinted in *Development: The Journal of the Society for International Development*, Vol 40, No 1.

2 Gustavo Esteva (1992), 'Development' in W. Sachs (ed), *The Development Dictionary: A Guide to Knowledge as Power*, London: Zed. Also G. Esteva and M. S. Prakash, *Hope at the Margins: Beyond Human Rights and Development*, London: Zed (forthcoming, 1998).

3 Mike Powell and David Seddon (1997), Editorial, *Review of African Political Economy*, Number 71.

4 See, for example, the following entries in the Annotated Bibliography to this volume: Franz Fanon, Paulo Freire, Rajni Kothari, Julius Nyerere, Vandana Shiva, Ngugi wa Thiong'o.

5 Powell and Seddon, op.cit.

Development and patronage

Melakou Tegegn

The predominance and consequences of globalisation 'from above' compel us to raise fundamental questions, the answers to which (with the further implication that these are 'universally' applicable) have long been taken for granted: questions that could not and cannot be answered through the prism of old paradigms, questions which do not even interest the powerful, for they are 'less curious than the powerless ... because they think they have all the answers. *And they do*. But not to the questions that the powerless are asking' (Kumar, 1996:2). Yet the paradigm and practice of the powerful still prevail: the chariot of modernisation and industrialisation is galloping ahead at an alarming speed, the market has broken through the walls of the previously impenetrable fortresses of nature and of indigenous peoples: the Amazon, the Mekong, and now the Nile. The world has surrendered to the universal mode, to the dominant paradigm and discourse on development. And it is precisely the validity of this discourse that we will explore here: its ethics, and whether or not it answers the many questions that humanity is raising.

The dominant discourse

The dominant paradigm on development is based on the science and technology whose power and influence was made possible through military might, colonisation of the South, domination and occupation, violence against women, and destruction of nature and the environment. Very few people question whether this science is ethical and natural, which is why the dominant discourse on development and its various related facets also goes unquestioned. The very framework of our intellectual development, which has been informed and shaped by the same dominant discourse, does not permit that. The South has also yielded to this discourse, this world-view or cosmology. As Kumar aptly put it (ibid., p.3):

The 'South' has, for too long, accepted a world view that has hegemonised its cultures, decided its development model, defined its aesthetic categories, outlined its military face, determined its science and technology, its nuclear options. A cosmology constructed of what has come to be known as 'universal' values; a cosmology whose philosophical, ideological and political roots were embedded in the specific historical context of the culture of the West .

Without necessarily implying that these are the antithesis of the dominant paradigm, the corollary is that the existence of various knowledge systems — sciences if you like — must be recognised, along with the acceptance that Northern science is just one such knowledge system, and not *the* science, *the* paradigm, and *the* discourse.

The subject in the process of social development must be people, for the essence of development must be to improve people's standard of living. A change for the better first of all implies the consent of the people. What constitutes a *better standard of living* must be defined by the people themselves. However, people have until now often been dragged into a definition and measurement of the process of social development, using the yardstick of Northern values. Consequently, people's own social and traditional organisations have been seen as archaic, traditional values as backward, and their knowledge systems as 'unscientific'. People were expected and even taught to abandon their traditional organisational systems, their values, and so on. In short, changing their identities was the precondition for the kind of 'development' prescribed by the North. Thus, people's authentic institutions or associations — the family, councils of elders, religious institutions, credit associations, their values and customs — were (and still are) supposed to be replaced by alien 'modern' forms.

Development revisited

What, then, is development? What does it mean? Who defines it? What are the criteria used to define development or under-development? And what are the yardsticks (and whose are they?) used to determine whether or not a given society is 'developed' or 'under-developed'? These are crucial questions that urgently need to be raised at this historical conjuncture, in a world whose very existence is threatened by the alarming way in which its ecology and environment are being destroyed.

Another factor is the collapse of the 'development' models that were attempted in the South, compounded by the post-Cold War social amnesia in the North. Since 1949, when the term 'under-development' entered the official discourse, development has always been one-sidedly understood to mean economic or material growth. The UN and other international bodies, as well as political establishments and academic institutions, took this skewed definition for granted. Some went further still, pointing to the 'indicators of development', and

taking GNP as the principal, if not the only, such indicator. In a nutshell, development = modernisation = industrialisation.

The Northern notion of development has characteristics that derive from its own historical evolution — starting with the industrial revolution and colonial expansion — and so has cultural and ethical foundations that are peculiar to the North. This evolution and the resulting cultural and ethical foundations are either absent from, or quite different in, the South. Prior to colonialism, Southern peoples had various political, social, and economic organisations, each based on their own cultural and ethical foundations. They differ significantly from those of the North. In the colonial era, however, Southern identities were forced to change in order to satisfy the economic and political motives of the colonial powers. In a compelling deconstruction of the Northern discourse on development, Gustavo Esteva notes:

When the metaphor returned to the vernacular, it acquired a violent colonising power, soon employed by the politicians. It converted history into a program: a necessary and inevitable destiny. The industrial mode of production, which was no more than one, among many, forms of social life, became the definition of the terminal stage of a unilinear way of social evolution ... Thus history was reformulated in Western terms (Esteva, 1992:19).

Or, as Sailendranath Ghosh has it,

countries which ought to be regarded as maldeveloped — which waste resources and degrade man — are called developed on account of their elitist consumerism, military power and technology for maximum exploitation of man and Nature (Ghosh, 1988:43).

When the term 'under-development' was coined after the second world war, it essentially reinforced the hegemonic content in the Northern beliefs and definitions of what 'development' is about. But what about the values in other cultures? What are the definitions and indicators of 'development' in the South, in other social forms? Are material abundance, economic prosperity, or technological 'advancement' the only indicators of 'development'? What about richness in human values as reflected in family, social, gender, racial, and ethnic relations? In many (pre-industrial) Southern cultures, there are indeed social and ethical values that are considered to be proper norms in a human society, and which could just as well be taken as indicators of 'development'. There is no point in pitching the values of the North ('developed'(?), industrial, rich) against those of the South ('under-developed'(?), pre-industrial, poor), or *vice versa*. Inasmuch as the North seeks recognition and respect for *its* values, similarly it must respect and recognise those of the South. Dichotomies need to give way to mutual recognition, though without denying the universality of certain human values which are pertinent and central to human development: values such as gender equality, liberty and the right to free expression, ethnic equality, and harmony among peoples.

In this respect, despite its weaknesses, the *Human Development Report* published annually by the UNDP since 1993, and the Human Development Index it uses to indicate levels of 'development' country by country, are quite a break from the previous discourse on the determinants of development indicators. It constitutes a major breakthrough in the process of re-thinking development paradigms. If dichotomies are to be avoided and recognition of values in all cultures is to prevail, development should be taken as a totality of people's material well-being on the one hand, and the flourishing of ethical and cultural values on the other. Can one speak of 'development' in terms of material abundance, if this is accompanied by ethical and cultural impoverishment? And *vice versa*? Ethical impoverishment is worth emphasising here, for it is the source of misunderstanding that often lead to conflicts among peoples.

Globalisation

With the completion of the globalisation process, the formula development = modernisation = industrialisation has added one more element: 'marketisation'. Globalisation and 'the end of the Cold War' are not empty phrases. They signify not only the emergence of a unipolar world dominated by the market system, but also the whole chain of changes that have resulted. These changes are occurring within the very structures of society, within the sovereignty of the nation-State in the South, with the emergence of new class fractions associated with and dependent on the global market system, and in a global political context (and UN system) dominated by the USA.

In concrete terms, certain social, political, and economic problems are aggravated as the result of the globalisation process and the pre-domination of the market. Poverty in general has been globalised, turning hundreds of millions of people in the South into paupers, and rendering many millions of people in the North unemployed. In today's world, poverty is no longer the exclusive identity of the South: it is also widespread in the North. The feminisation of poverty characterises this globalised poverty, and is the other side of the same coin. The position of women in many parts of the world has worsened (as many UN reports demonstrate), and violence against them has continued unabated, with the outbreak of wars and conflicts and the intensification of trafficking in women and sex tourism. Environmental degradation and the disturbance of the ecosystem have reached such alarming levels that the future of human civilisation is now seriously in question. Ethnic tension and conflicts have become the hallmarks of the late twentieth century, with a deterioration in the conditions of indigenous peoples everywhere. Complementing this crisis in the prevailing development paradigm, the imposed secularism of the nation-State in the South — imitating the modernisation process of the North, in the name of 'development' — has re-kindled certain traditional and local values that have in turn contributed to the spread of religious fundamentalism. The economic policy prescriptions (medicines!) and conditionalities imposed by the World Bank and the International Monetary Fund (IMF) have thrown millions and millions of people around the globe into poverty. *This is the reality of the world at the dawn of the twenty-first century: the reality of globalisation and the post-Cold War era.*

If the Northern modernisation processes that took place in previous centuries broke every national frontier through gunboat diplomacy, or through direct colonisation and occupation, the current process of modernisation — peddled through globalisation — has a different face. Today, it is the mega-financial institutions that impose their will through Southern governments and nation-States. From the tiny island of Fiji in the Pacific to Ghana in West Africa, the peoples of the South are subjected to the economic medicine of structural adjustment programmes which make, among other things, devaluation of national currencies, privatisation schemes, and the withdrawal of State subsidies and State intervention in the economy absolute conditions for receipt of IMF or World Bank loans. The consequence of this is the integration and absorption of Southern national economies into the global market system, as well as the complete abolition of some public services, and withdrawals or cutbacks in overall public spending, government subsidies, and social-security systems. These cuts have seriously affected the condition of women and the quality of health systems and public education. With the integration of their national economies into the global market system, countries of the South must then submit to the dictates or domination of the Bretton Woods Institutions (BWIs) — the Bank and the Fund — and now the new World Trade Organisation (WTO).

The South is also victim to the political 'rationale' of the BWIs. 'Political stability' is advanced without qualification as the 'precondition for development'. Examples such as those of the 'tigers' (Singapore, South Korea, Hong Kong, and Taiwan), Indonesia, and a handful of other countries in the South are cited as illustrations. Democracy and human rights are almost, in some cases, portrayed as 'luxuries' for the South. In other words, it is the powers in the North that know what people in the South need; and political issues such as democracy, human rights, and women's rights are luxuries that only the 'developed' and 'civilised' North can afford.

Such problems are further aggravated by the actual processes of globalisation, which are affecting mainly the peoples of the South. But what happens as a consequence of nuclear tests in the South Pacific or nuclear waste-dumping somewhere else affects people, and the poor in particular, everywhere. The trafficking of women and sex tourism know no frontiers. Nor does AIDS. Thus, globalisation has also made inter-dependence the reality of today's world. The prevailing form of globalisation is that which comes 'from above'. Inter-dependence has, however, compelled many forces within civil societies the world over to explore ways of getting together in response to this process. Networks have been formed, forums have been opened, social movements have spread, and many NGOs are still emerging in many countries. This is a natural response by civil societies to the consequences of the policies of those who dominate the world today: a kind of globalisation 'from below'.

Beyond inter-dependence, globalisation has also brought new issues, new questions, and new problems on to the development agenda. What is crucial within the context of these emerging questions and challenges is the role that civil-society organisations in the North can play in constructing and developing a new and genuine form of South-North cooperation and solidarity. If it is true that it was not only a poor country, Vietnam, which defeated the aggression committed against it by the USA, but also the anti-war solidarity movement in the cities of the North and in the USA in particular, it is also true that the struggle against globalisation 'from above' cannot be won without the active participation of civil-society organisations in the North.

This has now reached the level of necessity in order to create a united political response to the reality of globalised problems. At the level of consciousness too, it is vital to go more deeply into contextualising the problems that are arising in the globalisation process, which are in reality the problems faced by oppressed peoples everywhere. It is crucial for NGOs, social movements, and other organisations of civil society to adopt such a perspective. Because, in developing a strategy, it has become imperative to analyse one's own particular problem from the global perspective, and the global problem from the local perspective. The reality of globalisation compels us to broaden our scope, to reinforce our consciousness and knowledge, and raise these to a higher level.

Development and gender

The contemporary world had never seen such a fascinating social awakening as it did in the 1960s and 1970s, particularly in the women's movement, and the emergence of feminist-inspired thinking and paradigms, which later led to the development of a gender perspective. Without doubt, this noble movement has contributed greatly to changing perceptions of relations between the sexes, however modestly, throughout the world. However, despite all the legislation of governments, the UN declarations and resolutions, and the global forums on women, the position of women has not yet substantially changed. On the contrary, according to recent issues of the UNDP *Human Development Report*, the conditions of women in many parts of the world have in fact worsened. Assuming that all other existing conditions remain unchanged, the condition of women will certainly continue to deteriorate.

Though the discourse on women's equality continues, the gender component within the wider discourse on civil society and social development must come to occupy a determinant position. 'Structurally', civil society is that part of society which is located outside the realm of the political power (the State). Women, both numerically and as those who have been disempowered since the dawn of history, constitute a profoundly important and organic component within any democratic civil society. The language and definition of the term 'development' must start with changes and improvement in the conditions of women, who are the most relegated — yet crucial — element not only of civil society, but of human civilisation itself. If development means change for the better, its definition must start with what constitutes the better: a change and improvement in the

condition of women. We have to start with the question: what must change? What is universal in this respect is the degraded position of women in society, both because their material conditions of existence are inadequate, and because of men's attitude towards women, and the attitude of women towards themselves. Patriarchy must disappear both from the minds of men and of women. The injustice, the physical and psychological violence unleashed against women, originate from and have their roots in patriarchy. Patriarchy is not just oppressive and exploitative; it is also violent. It comes under the guise of tradition, custom, culture, and even religion: all justifying the degradation of women and the violence against them. Consciously or unconsciously, this is violence by the community against women and, therefore, against itself. This is what underdevelopment is, and it is precisely this underdevelopment which is universal, from the Medina of Sana'a in Yemen to Harlem in the USA, from Cape Town in South Africa to Reykjavik in Iceland.

If we opt for a humane society, development and democracy must be defined and measured according to positive changes firstly in the *position* of women, and secondly in the *attitude* towards women of men and women alike. This is fundamental, for it constitutes a truly radical change. The most difficult thing for human beings to change is themselves: liberating themselves from the thinking transmitted from the past in the name of tradition. Development means that each man, among other things, should start thinking differently and in a positive way about the women whose lives are closely linked with his.

This should not be taken as an appeal for change to conform with Western thinking, for in this sense the West itself is still underdeveloped. The position of women in the West and the attitude of society towards them is still deplorable, to say the least. In the case of Africa, this patriarchal and traditional outlook has been reinforced by colonial intervention, and now by the injection of 'modernisation' and 'modernity' through institutions such as the IMF.

Development and human rights

If there is one area where the dominance of the development discourse is glaringly obvious, it is that of human rights. The prevailing discourse on human rights is historically specific to the period of the European Enlightenment, with its ideological and philosophical foundations in liberal thought. Its material foundation is the private industrial mode of production and the market economy. Private interest, the interest of the individual, private profits, and competition were its creed. Equating with and restricting the concept of human rights simply to the right of the individual has its historical basis in the rise of capitalist industrialisation. This discourse is advanced by the powers that currently dominate the economic, social, and political life of the industrialised societies. As Corinne Kumar has rightly pointed out, the dominant discourse is and was 'a partial dialogue within a civilisation' (ibid., 11).

Today, the Western discourse on human rights has become the global language, having negated other civilisations, values, philosophies, and State systems particularly in Africa, Asia, the Americas, the Arab World, and so on, firstly through colonial conquests and now through the globalisation process. The values in most civilisations of the South that rested not only on respect for the rights of the individual, but equally on the well-being and interest of the collective on the one hand, and on respect for the environment on the other, were scrapped by the expansion of industrialisation and the market. In much of the South, therefore, the rights and interests of the collective are as important as those of the individual, since it is the collective and not the individual which plays the most decisive role in life in the South. This should in no way be taken as a defence of 'tradition', inasmuch as 'tradition' in this context is not being seen in opposition to 'modernity'. On the contrary, in 'traditional' societies, there are also patriarchy, violence, and repression that should be abhorred.

Human rights are, however, generally considered as being the agenda of the South. This assumption denies the existence of human-rights violations in the North. Yet human-rights violations in the North constitute a serious problem, as the capacity of citizens to live decently as human beings gets weakened by the day. There were 40,000 homeless people in Chicago alone in 1986; there is a seven per cent rate of illiteracy among Afro-Americans just in Mississippi; and the increasing problem of unemployment is regarded by the Chicago school of economists as insoluble. If a great many citizens of countries in the North cannot live as human beings because of want, hunger, homelessness, illiteracy, and other material needs, then what is this if not a violation of human rights?

Equality and partnership in development

One relic of the dominant discourse is reflected in what passes as 'partnership in development'. After the 1939–1945 war, the North was categorised as 'developed' and the South as 'under-developed'. 'Logically' it followed that it was the South which needed 'development', and that the North would help the South to 'develop'. This was somewhat tempered after the 1960s, and was followed by claims of 'equality and partnership' in the 'development' process in the South. The question of 'equality and partnership in development in the North' has never been considered, for the existence of under-development in the North has not yet been recognised.

However, globalisation 'from above' (of the market) has made inter-dependence — something beyond solidarity — a necessity on the part of the globally marginalised, who are increasingly being made dispensable for the sake of industrialisation, expansion of the market, and 'modernisation'. Those who are involved in the development process, in the struggle against poverty, against violence against women, against the destructive exploitation of the natural environment increasingly realise the inter-dependence of global civil society. This has been translated into the formation of various global and regional networks and forums. Much hope is inspired by this greater degree of contact within global civil society, the process of globalisation 'from below'.

However, this global civil society is a conglomeration of great diversities. There is a long way to go before a unity of social action can be achieved. One such constraint is the lop-sided view concerning equality and partnership in development. Contemporary inter-dependence has meant that a development project has changed from being the concern of a given locality or region into being of wider concern to global civil society. For example, the social movement against French nuclear tests in the South Pacific is no longer the concern only of the people of the Pacific; an environmental project to preserve the forests in the highlands of Ethiopia has positive impact in the Sahel as a whole; and so on. The fight against material poverty in the South also has a positive impact on the North. Such inter-dependence renders the 'donor–recipient' dichotomy obsolete. Partnership in development is no longer an expression of solidarity, but has become an imperative: equality between 'donors' and 'recipients' is now an absolute necessity.

References

Esteva, G. (1992) in *The Development Dictionary*, ed. Sachs, London: Zed Books

Ghosh, S. (1988) 'A plea for re-examining the concepts of development and reorienting science and technology', in *Global Development and Environment Crisis — Has Humankind a Future?*, Penang, Malaysia: Sahabat Alam

Kumar, C. (1996) *South Wind: On the Universality of the Human Rights Discourse*, Tunis: El Taller

African libraries and the consumption and production of knowledge

Paul Tiyambe Zeleza

Global village or feudal estate?

We live in the information age, so we are always told, in which information is apparently as vital as agriculture and industry once were. It is an age of infinite possibilities in education and scholarship, teaching and research, economic growth and political freedom; a brave new world blessed with the open intimacies of the village, where the boundaries of national isolation and intellectual provincialism are withering away, as knowledge expands in its relentless march towards human enlightenment. Extravagant claims, no doubt. Knowledge, as creed and commodity, as a proprietary privilege, reflects and reproduces the spatial and social divisions of power, old and new, material and ideological, between and within societies. The 'information highway' is a dangerous place for those on foot or riding rickety bicycles. It is designed for, and dominated by, those travelling courtesy of powerful and prestigious publishing systems and academic enterprises of the industrialised North, who churn out the bulk of the world's books, journals, databases, computers and software and other information technologies, and dictate laws on international copyright and intellectual property to the information-poor world. A harmonious global village it is not. A feudal estate, hierarchical and unequal, it may be.

What is Africa's position on this feudal estate? Where does it fit in the international political economy of knowledge production, dissemination, and consumption? To answer these questions we need to assess the development and state of the continent's basic infrastructures for creating and distributing knowledge: namely, the availability of publishing houses, technical expertise, printing facilities, electronic technologies, libraries, and capable writers. It is not enough, however, to bemoan the regional and social disparities in access to information, or to chronicle the unequal patterns of information acquisition, outreach, and infrastructure. We need to unravel the content, the value, of the information. What social good has it generated? To what extent has the explosion of information led to more enlightened human relations within and among nations? Is the 'information highway' all speed, noise, and fury leading nowhere, and leaving behind only data-glut and confusion? In short, we must interrogate the ethics of information, the social and political morality of knowledge creation, consumption, and content, and assess its record in bettering the human condition, not just materially, but in ennobling social relations, in uplifting the human spirit.

These are the issues discussed in this article.[1] The first part offers an overview of the challenges facing African academic and research libraries, crucial centres for the consumption and production of knowledge; and examines the band-aid solutions that have been tried, only to reinforce the continent's external dependency.[2] The second part argues that the plight of African research libraries as a crisis of scholarly communication cannot be adequately tackled without developing and improving local academic publishing and information-production capacities, to ensure the dissemination of knowledge that better reflects African realities. But we must avoid the pitfalls of either romanticising indigenous knowledge or turning library holdings into a fetish — for neither guarantees accessibility or enlightenment. Thus the challenges of producing and disseminating knowledge and information ultimately centre on questions of cultural democratisation and social responsibility. And these are not peculiarly African problems. They are universal.

The struggle for the bookshelves

African libraries carry a heavy colonial imprint, even in those regions with long traditions of literacy and libraries, such as Northern Africa, Ethiopia, and parts of Western and Eastern Africa, partly because virtually the whole continent (including Ethiopia between 1935 and 1941), was under colonial rule. After independence — a period that witnessed the fastest expansion of libraries in the continent's history — colonial traditions were reinforced by a scramble for modernisation that assumed a concomitant need for Westernisation. African libraries heedlessly borrowed their architecture, collections, bibliographic and classification systems, training and staffing structures from the North, without adequately tethering them to the stubborn local realities of poverty and illiteracy, on the one hand, and the rich media of oral culture and the voracious appetite for education, on the other.

Research and academic libraries were the least domesticated, much like the universities themselves, whose institutional lineages and intellectual loyalties lay overseas. All was well in the heady years immediately following independence, when healthy commodity prices and booming economies kept modernisation hopes alive. The tentacles of information-dependency grew tighter and thicker, despite the inchoate nationalist yearning for cultural decolonisation. Then from the mid-1970s many African countries fell into a spiral of recurrent recessions, which wreaked havoc on development ambitions, and left a trail of economic decline, social dislocation,

and political disaffection — problems that were exacerbated by the disastrous programmes of structural maladjustment. The bookshelves grew empty. 'Book hunger' joined the litany of Africa's other famines of development, democracy, and self-determination.

The impact of structural adjustment

The prevailing library and information system was in a crisis of self-reproduction and relevance. This is amply borne out by the 1993 survey of 31 university and research libraries in 13 African countries conducted by the American Association for the Advancement of Science (AAAS). All but three of the libraries reported a sharp drop in their subscriptions to journals from the mid-1980s. Among the worst-hit were the libraries of Addis Ababa University and the University of Nigeria, and the University of Yaoundé Medical Library, which in the late 1980s and early 1990s cancelled subscriptions to some 1,200, 824, and 107 journals respectively, owing to shortage of foreign exchange (Levey, 1993: 2-3). Currency devaluation, one of the linchpins of structural adjustment programmes, also took its toll on the buying power of libraries. As the Librarian of Abubakar Tafawa University said in 1993: 'at the current rate of 25 *naira* to the dollar, I should have about $229,000 for books. Ten years ago, I would have been swimming in dollars — for at $1.50 to *N*1, the same *naira* would have equalled over $8 million' (*ibid.*, 9). Compounding matters were unpredictable currency fluctuations which imposed further and unanticipated expenditures.

It was a fatal concoction, this combination of currency devaluations and fluctuations, together with the escalating cost in the price of journals and books. Today, it is common to find journals with annual subscriptions costing $1,000, especially in the sciences. One study estimates that serial costs in North America, from where African research libraries import many materials, increased 115 per cent between 1986 and 1994, and monograph costs rose by 55 per cent. As a result, serial acquisitions among members of the US-based Association of Research Libraries dropped by four per cent and monographs by 22 per cent (Birenbaum, 1995). If research libraries in the

North were feeling the chill, those in Africa caught pneumonia. The case of the University of Ibadan Library is all too typical. Its subscriptions plummeted from over 6,000 serials in 1983 to less than a tenth of that a decade later (Levey, 1993:3).

The three fortunate libraries that reported increases in the number of subscriptions — the University of Nairobi Medical Library, the National Mathematical Centre of Nigeria, and Abubakar Tafawa Balewa University — subscribed to no more than 200 journals each. Indeed, only seven libraries in the AAAS survey subscribed to more than 200 journals with internal funding. Of these, only three, led by the University of Zimbabwe Library with 1,578 journals paid through the library's budget, could boast more than 500 subscriptions. But even the latter saw its foreign-currency allocation decline from 65 per cent of the funds requested in 1989 to less than 40 per cent in 1991 (Levey, 1993: 4-5).

Aggravating the dire financial conditions in which the libraries found themselves were the ill-advised government taxes on imports of books and journals.[3] Bureaucratic red tape often makes matters worse: getting imported books out of customs can often take weeks, even months.

The universities themselves are also to blame. Their expenditure patterns are usually skewed in favour of salaries and privileges for the administrative elite, with their fleets of official cars, heavily subsidised housing, and numerous allowances: self-indulgent practices reminiscent of the corrupt political class. And so the universities seek to reproduce themselves, not as intellectual ivory towers, nor as locomotives of progress, but as the inert apparatus of the State, a mission that leaves little room for serious commitment to scholarly communication and critical pedagogy.

The dubious benefits of library aid

One response been growing reliance on donations of books and journals from charitable organisations and foreign governments and their agencies. The AAAS survey found that only five of the libraries subscribing to journals in 1993 did so exclusively with internal funding. The rest depended to varying degrees on donor support. Five were dependent for as much as 100 per cent,

and another five for 80 per cent and more. Four had neither donor support nor their own funding. 'Thus without external funding,' the AAAS report states, 'many libraries would have few current journals on their shelves. But donor support', it notes correctly, 'raises its own set of dilemmas, which revolve around the dreaded term "sustainability"' (Levey, 1993:19). The donors do not underwrite projects indefinitely, which makes it difficult to pursue a rational programme of journal acquisitions. For example, the University of Makerere Library reduced its subscriptions from 700 to 200 serials when grants from the Overseas Development Agency (ODA) and the European Community expired in 1991.

Another problem is that library aid, like all aid, has strings attached. 'Book presentations', Clow (1986:87) writes, 'are usually restricted to items published in the donor country ... training usually involves donor-country citizens as teachers; if a scholarship is awarded, the scholar usually travels to and spends most of the money in the donor country.' African libraries rarely choose the journals and books that they receive from the donors.[4] Predictable, also, is the fact that most of the journals donated are North American and European, not African.[5] In short, book aid tends to reinforce Africa's dependency on Western values, languages, discourses, and institutions. Reluctant to bite the hand that feeds them, many librarians keep quiet, even when the donations are irrelevant and inappropriate. In the process, the culture of silence and submission to imperialism, which is partly responsible for the African crisis in the first place, deepens. And so they meekly receive, and fill their shelves with, or quietly dispose of, propaganda materials from embassies, the discarded miscellanea of Western libraries, grimy, out-of-date texts, and publishers' remainders. By filling the bare shelves of African libraries, well-meaning, but sometimes misguided, philanthropists can display their altruism; and hard-nosed publishers can dispose of their unsold tomes, and thus save themselves warehouse charges and earn welcome tax relief.

From the 1970s, donors and international agencies, especially UNESCO, produced a series of training and information-development programmes. But most of these, Sturges and Neill

(1990:97) contend, 'failed to produce results commensurate with the attention that the information professions have paid to them'. They attribute the failure of UNESCO's national programmes of library and information development to erroneous assumptions, inadequate planning, and poor design, problems often exacerbated by the lack of State support, sparse infrastructures, and excessive duplication and rivalry among the donor agencies themselves. Similar challenges have hampered efforts by Africa-based organisations to develop regional information systems. The most well-known is the Pan-African Documentation and Information System (PADIS), begun in 1980 and administered by the Economic Commission for Africa (ECA). Its broad aims are to help African countries to strengthen their own internal information systems, and to set up a decentralised information network for the continent. While PADIS has made considerable progress, and publishes useful bibliographic indexes, especially concerning development, it certainly achieved far less in its first ten years than the investment of $160 million warranted, partly due to misguided emphasis on expensive information technologies for countries with poor telecommunications infrastructures.

The role of information technology

This is not to suggest that the latest information technologies should not be acquired, for not to do so would be to reinforce Africa's marginalisation. It is simply to point out that basic infrastructural development is essential, and that in themselves the advanced technologies offer no magic solution to the challenges of information dissemination and scholarly communication facing Africa. Many African research libraries, usually with donor support, are investing heavily in computer and CD-ROM capability, and electronic networking (AAS and AAAS, 1992). To its champions, the CD-ROM is a wonder-technology that is universally appropriate: not only can it hold huge amounts of data, it is durable, cheap to mail, requires no special handling, storage space, or telecommunication facilities, and can withstand climatic extremes, power cuts, and the ravages of insects and fungi. The potentialities of advanced

technologies for liberation and repression are in serious dispute (Kagan, 1992; Buschman, 1992). Lancaster (1978) urged developing countries to seize on the new technologies and leapfrog to electronic libraries, by-passing the book. His critics have argued that electronic information services in Africa benefit only a small, already privileged elite. African librarians, they assert, ought to be concentrating on helping the illiterate majority to learn to read and write (Mchombu, 1982; Olden, 1987; IFLA, 1995). Others argue for an integrated approach that combines improved information delivery to both the poor and the elites (Tiamiyu, 1989; Sturges and Neill, 1990).

The 1993 AAAS report found that all but five of the 31 libraries surveyed had computers, about half of them purchased locally, and most of them acquired through donor support. Nineteen libraries had CD-ROM capability, and two were expecting to acquire it by the end of 1993. African librarians have been keen to acquire CD-ROM technology 'for fear of being left behind', in the words of John Newa (1993:82), the Director of Library Services at the University of Dar es Salaam. At a 1993 workshop in Harare on new technologies for librarians from 17 libraries in 11 countries in eastern and southern Africa (including South Africa), 16 of whom were equipped with CD-ROMs, there was universal agreement on the importance of this technology, despite some of its perceived shortcomings. With a few exceptions, many of the libraries reported extensive use of the CD-ROM facilities. The University of Zambia Medical Library was even forced to ration time to 30 minutes per person. Most of the libraries in the AAAS report subscribed to databases in agriculture and medicine, mainly because of the interest of donors, who largely pay for the subscriptions in these fields. The notable exception was the library of Cheikh Anta Diop, which had a significant number of CD-ROM databases in the social sciences (Levey, 1993: 13–16).

Computers and CD-ROM technologies have breathed new life into Africa's ailing research library systems, although they pose their own problems, and reinforce some old ones. Lack of relevant technical expertise locally and among librarians often leads to poor choice of product, and installation and maintenance difficulties. One study reports, for example, that 'the librarian of the University of Ghana Medical School had no one in Ghana to whom to turn when he had trouble installing his CD-ROM drive, for his is the first library with CD-ROM in the country. Ultimately he called New York to receive instructions over the phone' (Levey, 1991:12). But long-distance advice can be costly and inappropriate, as the librarian of the University of Zimbabwe Medical School discovered after buying a non-compatible CD drive 'on the basis of advice from our New York software vendors' (Levey, 1991:12).

These technologies of course do not come cheap, so the question of funding remains. Besides the one-off equipment costs, which rise each time local currencies are devalued, there is the high recurrent cost of subscription to data-bases. Training costs can also be high and recur-rent, especially since the technology is growing and changing rapidly. It is essential to budget for CD-ROM subscriptions for the long run, because subscribers are usually allowed to use the databases only for the duration of the subscription and may be requested to return the disks should their subscriptions run out — unlike journals, which a library keeps when its subscription lapses (Levey, 1992). Not surprisingly, there is report-edly a handful of libraries with CD-ROMs who do not use them because they have no funds to purchase subscriptions. Of the 16 libraries with CD-ROMs surveyed by the AAAS in 1991, only four indicated they had funding for subscriptions in the future. Nor do literature searches guarantee the users access to the documents identified. Given the inadequacy of many African research libraries' serials collections, bibliographic data-bases that do not contain abstracts are virtually useless (Patrikios, 1992: 30–7). Few donors include document delivery as an integral part of their grants for database subscriptions, and supplying photocopies from Europe and North America, as is sometimes done, is costly and cumbersome. The document-delivery barriers may ease as full-text literature is routinely published on disk as well as in print form.

The struggle for knowledge

African librarians are fully aware of these problems, and many realise the importance of national and regional cooperation, although declared intentions tend to predominate over concrete action.[6] But even if the question of access to citations and documents were resolved, Africa's knowledge base would not necessarily improve, for these databases — like the bulk of the journals and books imported into most of the continent's libraries — primarily contain North-ern scholarship. Production costs for CD-ROM databases are still prohibitive for any aspiring African publisher, although efforts are being made to create local databases.[7] Besides, the publisher would have to develop extensive scholarly, marketing, and support networks. Northern database publishers are still largely unwilling or unable to incorporate bibliographic records from the South. By the mid-1980s there were an estimated 700 databases of direct concern to Africa located outside the continent; the figure has most probably risen with the explosion in electronic communications since then (Seeley, 1986). Not only are these databases difficult to access within Africa itself, but their input of African research and publications is abysmal. For example, fewer than one per cent of more than 36,000 items on Africa contained in the FRANCIS data file (with one million items in total), produced by the French Centre National de la Recherche Scientifique as of March 1986, were published in Africa (Sturges and Neill, 1990: 64-5). In the case of even the best of these data-bases, FAO's Agricultural Information System (AGRIS), only 25 per cent of the content derives from the developing countries.

The need to reclaim African studies

The marginality of African knowledge is evident even in scholarly communication networks that call themselves Africanist. Overseen by gate-keepers located in well-endowed universities, the Africanist intellectual system, firmly rooted in a Western epistemological order and an academic culture driven by a ruthless ethos of 'publish or perish', and consisting of multinational publishing houses, university presses, journals, peer-review networks, citation and bibliographic conventions, has little room for alien views, voices, and visions emanating from Africa itself. On this scholarly treadmill, Africa appears nothing more than a research object to verify faddish theories that emerge with predictable regularity in the channel-surfing intellectualism of Northern academies. Research on five leading Africanist social science and humanities journals published in Britain, Canada, and the USA showed that between 1982 and 1992 only 15 per cent of their articles and 10 per cent of their book reviews were by Africans based in Africa. African authors based in the West accounted for a further 9 per cent of the articles and 5 per cent of the reviews (Zeleza, forthcoming).

Detailed analysis of the contents of Africanist publications would be revealing. To what extent do their themes engage the realities and priorities of the communities studied and the genuine research interests of the scholars from those communities, as opposed to research orientations dictated by the consultancy syndrome or careerist calculations in situations where publishing in Western scholarly media carries more weight than publishing within Africa? There is some evidence to suggest that the agendas of African and Africanist research communities have grown more divergent over the years — a trend which is attributable to changing conditions for African studies in the North and the scholarly enterprise in Africa. On the one hand, Africanist scholars spend less time than they used to in Africa, whether in research or teaching, partly because of funding difficulties, reduced salaries in African universities, and fewer teaching opportunities resulting from the successful Africanisation of faculties. On the other hand, the proportion of African scholars studying for higher degrees in the North, especially in the social sciences and humanities, has also fallen, because of declining need, lack of financial resources, the unattractiveness of academic careers, and growing immigration restrictions. Contacts are especially poor for what Mkandawire (1995) calls the 'third generation' of African scholars, a point echoed by Guyer (1995) with reference to the younger crop of aspiring North American Africanists.

Mkandawire, CODESRIA's executive secretary and a keen observer of the two scholarly communities, has noted, for example (1995:4), that in the 1980s, while many Africanists were fashionably bemoaning or applauding the 'exit' of peasants and other exploited social classes from arenas dominated by the authoritarian post-colonial State, 'African social scientists moved in a different direction, casting attention more towards the study of social movements and democracy'. Currently, post-modernism is casting its spell on many in the Africanist fraternity, and some are anxiously covering their mouldy African data with its ephemeral fragrance, forgetting proclamations they made in the 1960s that Africa was modernising, in the 1970s that it was under-developing, and later that modes of production were being articulated. Sleeping its way through the lost 1980s, Africa somehow woke up in the 1990s to find itself in a post-modernist universe — or it should have, we are told (Parpart, 1995). To many African scholars on the continent, such arcane preoccupations seem the nadir of intellectual solipsism and decadence. According to Aina (1995:2), the crisis of African Studies in North America and Europe is creating

a process of intellectual reproduction about Africa that is characterized by sterility, outdated facts and information, casual and ad hoc observation, name-calling and sometimes wild speculation. It is our argument here that for an up to date, realistic, correct and appropriate ... understanding of Africa, the most appropriate and relevant source is that scholarship and production emanating from or still directly linked to the continent in terms of research experience and reflection; from this living and challenging source and expression, no amount of post-modernist, post-industrialist, post-Marxist or 'post-Nativist' conceptualization or discourse can take away the relevance, immediacy and centrality.

The inescapable conclusion is that importing knowledge from abroad is no panacea. And for Africa to depend on external sources for knowledge about itself is a cultural and economic travesty of monumental proportions. To use a phrase from the under-development paradigm,

African libraries may grow from buying or receiving donations of tons of journals and books, and they may acquire the latest information technologies and the largest databases; but without actually developing, without expanding and strengthening the continent's capacities for authentic and sustainable knowledge-creation, information-generation, and data-collection. More often than not, knowledge produced about Africa from elsewhere is distorted or irrelevant, and importing databases or receiving donations serves to strengthen the ties of intellectual dependency. Sturges and Neill (1990:79) irreverently suggest that 'many of the donations that do arrive would be far better if they were pulped. This might at least provide some new paper, a basic resource which Africa needs more urgently than other countries' cast-off books.'

The real challenge, then, is not simply to fill empty library shelves and acquire gadgets for faster information-retrieval, but to produce the knowledge in the first place; for Africa to study, read, and know itself, to define itself to itself and to the rest of the world, and to see that world through its own eyes and not the warped lenses of others. There is no substitute for a vigorous intellectual system, of which publishing is an integral part. As I have noted elsewhere (Zeleza, 1994:238):

Only by developing and sustaining our own publishing outlets can there emerge truly African intellectual traditions and communities capable of directing and controlling the study of Africa, of defining African problems and solutions, realities and aspirations, of assessing our achievements and failures, our pasts and futures, and of seeing ourselves in our own image, not through the distortions and fantasies of others. Publishing is critical not only for the cultural identities of nations, peoples, classes, and groups. It provides the material basis for producing, codifying, circulating and consuming ideas, which, in turn, shape the organisation of productive activities and relations in society.

African publishing: constraints and opportunities

The challenges of publishing in Africa and other Third World regions are well known. They include poor infrastructure (in particular, shortages of skilled editors, designers, distribution experts, and readily available and cheap supplies of printing equipment and paper), as well as low literacy rates, language problems, and meagre incomes and purchasing power — problems which have been exacerbated by the recurrent recessions. Promotion and marketing, at home and abroad, remains a critical hurdle for many African publishers (Zell, 1995: 16-18). For instance, Nyariki and Makotsi (1995:11) found that the promotional and marketing activities undertaken by many Kenyan publishers are ineffective and unprofessional, because they lack trained staff. Moreover, widespread government intolerance and censorship in many countries only make matters worse. Nor does the existence of relatively small and fragile academic communities help, especially for scholarly publishing. And poorly capitalised indigenous publishers must often compete with large multinational publishing companies, and heavily subsidised State-owned publishing houses.[8]

These constraints are real and serious, but they are not insurmountable. Literacy rates have risen remarkably in many countries, and 'the much publicised myth that the African mind is orally-oriented and therefore Africans do not read' is becoming more threadbare as evidence mounts that a lot of people actually read for pleasure: Nyariki and Makotsi (1995:11) demonstrate that 'a majority 39% of consumers buy books because of a love of reading'. They also show that the number of indigenous publishers in Kenya doubled to 72 between 1974 and 1994 and that local publishers were producing 60 per cent of the books on the local market. These trends are confirmed by Hans Zell (1993:373), a seasoned observer of the African publishing scene, who states that 'despite the overall gloomy picture ... new indigenous imprints continue to mushroom all over Africa, and some privately owned firms have shown a great deal of imaginative entrepreneurial skill in the midst of adversity'. And the formation of the African Books Collective (ABC) by African publishers in 1989 to undertake the joint promotion and distribution of African books outside the continent, and of the African Publishers' Network (APNET) in 1992 to encourage intra-African publishing and trade in books, underscores the determination of African publishers to forge ahead.[9]

Libraries must do their part. They constitute the backbone of scholarly publishing. In many parts of the world, including the industrialised countries, libraries provide the major market for scholarly products. In fact, in the USA, despite relatively high academic salaries and a large professorate, it is library purchases, not subscriptions by individuals, that sustain journals. Often libraries generate up to 90 per cent or more of the income of journals, especially in the medical and scientific areas. Having fed for so long on Western imports and donations of information materials and technologies, African libraries have not always ventured with enough appetite to acquire local publications. For their part, publishers bred on the captive school-textbook market are not always aggressive enough in promoting their wares. At the Harare workshop mentioned above, publishers and librarians took each other to task (Patrikios and Levey, 1993:3):

Several publishers stated that few African imprints can be found in African libraries because librarians are reluctant to order materials, preferring instead to purchase books from England or the United States. Nana Tau (librarian of Fort Hare University) countered by telling of her experience in attempting to obtain information on African imprints in order to place an order for her library. The lack of response from the African publishers whom she wrote requesting catalogues forced her to place orders overseas.

On another occasion the Librarian at the University of Makerere pointed out that 'most of the African journals are possibly not known by teaching staff who recommend titles to be subscribed by the library' (quoted in Levey, 1993:11). Unfortunately, he may have been correct. It is a sad fact that in many African universities the processes of hiring and promoting staff and allocating research grants are firmly tied to the legitimation structures of Western scholarship. Familiarity with Western intellectual fads, and publication in the restricted Western scholarly media, bestow upon the lucky few precious reputational capital that can be traded for lucrative consultancies and overseas visiting professorships and conferences. Local journals become publication outlets of last resort, repositories of second-rate scholarship.

This must change. African intellectuals need to shed their inferiority complexes about their own work by publishing, without apologies, in journals they control; by reading and citing each other; by demonstrating a greater faith in their own understanding of their complex and fast-changing societies — for no one else will do that for them. They cannot continue being unwelcome guests at other people's intellectual tables. Through their reward structures, facilities, and ethos, universities should provide the major sources for intellectual production and markets for scholarly products. Where the scholarly communities are small, cooperative ventures in regional journal publication should be encouraged. The mission, always, must be to promote the highest standards of research and scholarly exchange, to repossess the study of Africa, to define African realities, to understand and appreciate the African world with all the intensity, intelligence, and integrity it deserves.

Conclusion

The manufacturing and distribution of scholarly knowledge and information is a major commercial and technological enterprise involving publishers, libraries, educational institutions, and communications companies, linked in elaborate networks requiring vast resources. The news that we have entered a post-material age in which words matter more than goods is exaggerated, but the importance of information technologies in the development process cannot be denied. But what kind of information, produced by and for whom?

One of the factors behind the information explosion in the Western countries, especially in North America, is the pressure to publish, the centrality of publications and citations in the academic enterprise. Publications have become screening mechanisms for hiring, promotion, tenure, and granting procedures. The system rewards those who generate large amounts of scholarly literature, however insignificant its intellectual contribution. Indeed, piles of paper are churned out to be listed and indexed rather than read. And so scholarly information doubles in volume every seven years. A decade and half ago it was doubling every 15 years (Birenbaum, 1995). Information becomes an absolute good, an end itself, an intolerant, insatiable god that constantly spews data, 'hyperfacts' that require more powerful databases to keep track of the existing databases (Roszak, 1993:4). In the process, knowledge becomes incidental, a forgotten atavism. As the information glut grows, there is ever more pressure for excessive specialisation. Meanwhile, as the high priests of the Information Age pray at the altar of citations and chant 'jargons of an almost unimaginable rebarbativeness ... society as a whole drifts without direction or coherence. Racism, poverty, ecological ravages, disease, and an appallingly widespread ignorance: these are left to the media and the odd political candidate during an election campaign' (Said, 1993:303).

Thus beneath the apparent munificence of the Western academy, behind the spiralling mountains of information, lies a profound shift away from human connectedness, from meaningful social conversation; there is a yawning alienation from the gravity of human existence, from history. An almost infantile fascination with the innate and quantifiable, not the poetry of life, of words, seems to have taken over. The availability of more information is not in itself a guarantee of a better society. As Olden (1987:301) reminds us:

the availability of information does not mean that use can be or will be made of it; that those who do use it are capable or willing to learn from it; or that what they learn will be used for the benefit of others. Taken together, United States libraries house what is probably the most comprehensive collection of recorded information and knowledge about other countries held by any nation in the world. Has the increase in the size of this collection since World War II been paralleled by

an increase in the number of better foreign-policy decisions made by various administrations over the same period?

And one could add: are North Americans much better informed about the rest of the world? Indeed, has more information helped them significantly to transcend their own division of race, ethnicity, class, and gender? Will access to the Internet in every home and to a 500 TV-channel universe do it? Or will that simply lead to more fragmentation, to further descent into the abyss of cultural banality so evident in North American popular television today?

What, in short, do the terms 'information-rich' and 'information-poor', which are so carelessly bandied about, actually mean in terms of the content of human relationships, the quality of social life, as embodied in the information being manufactured and consumed? To be sure, Africa needs to produce more information; its academic institutions need to reorganise themselves to encourage and reward scholarly production and productivity; and its libraries need to collect and make this information more accessible within and outside the continent. But the processes of production, acquisition, retrieval, and outreach cannot be ends in themselves, if the dangers of information over-production and overload, currently engulfing the Western world, are to be avoided. Africa must indeed repossess the word. But whose word, and to what ultimate purpose? It must be to elevate, not debase, our humanity.

Notes

1 This is a revised version of a paper originally presented at the International Book Fair and Library Conference, Göteborg, Sweden, 26-29 October 1995. My thanks to Al Kagan (Africana Librarian, the University of Illinois at Urbana-Champaign), Dr John Newa (Librarian at the University of Dar es Salaam), and Karin von Schlesbrügge of the Swedish International Development Agency for their comments, and to Tunde Brimah for research assistance.

2 The wider questions of the creation of knowledge and the provision of information for the popular classes in the urban or rural areas are not addressed here. For a detailed study of the provision of information to rural African communities, see IFLA (1995).

3 An interesting example is that of Côte d'Ivoire, where the Telecommunications and Postal Ministry was privatised. The AAAS stopped sending free journals to the university library, because the latter could not afford to pay the ministry the levies charged on the journals! (Levey, 1993:9).

4 Many of those concerned about book dumping in the Third World have suggested that donations schemes should be request-led. See Abid (1992).

5 A remarkable exception is the programme initiated by the International African Institute, which in the early 1990s launched a project to distribute 12 African serials, which were selected after consultations with African publishers and research libraries.

6 Only in South Africa do the efforts to integrate library systems and resources seem serious, for instance the Western Cape Cooperative Project and the Committee on Library Cooperation in Natal.

7 The Zimbabwe and Zambia Medical libraries, for example, in collaboration with other countries in Africa, are producing an *African Index Medicus*, while the Bunda College of Agriculture in Malawi has created a bibliographic database of Malawi's maize research.

8 The multinational publishing companies can be quite opportunistic. For example, they all closed their businesses in Tanzania during the 1980s financial crisis and 'returned in the 1990s when they heard that there would be an allocation of US$60 million from the World Bank for educational suppliers'! (Mcharazo 1995:245)

9 For a discussion of these organisations and their activities, see Zeleza 1994; and the 1993-95 issues of the *Bellagio Publishing Network Newsletter*, published on behalf of the donors which support African publishing; APNET's organ, *African Publishing Review*; and *The African Book Publishing Record*.

References

AAS and AAAS (1992) *Electronic Networking in Africa: Advancing Science and Technology for Development*, Nairobi: African Academy of Sciences and the American Association for the Advancement of Science

Abid, A. (1992) 'Improving access to scientific literature in developing countries: a Unesco programme review', *IFLA Journal*, 18/4: 315–24

Aina, T. A. (1995) 'Library Acquisitions of African Books: An Academic Publisher's Viewpoint', paper presented to the APNET Open Forum: Library Acquisition of African Books, Harare, 2 August

Birenbaum, R. (1995) 'Scholarly communication under siege', *University Affairs*, Association of Universities and Colleges of Canada, August–September: 6

Buschman, J. (1992) 'A response', *Progressive Librarian*, 5:51–3

Clow, D. (1986) 'Aid and development — the context of library-related aid', *Libri*, 36/2:85–97

Guyer, J. L. (1995) *A Perspective on African Studies in the United States*, Report Submitted to the Ford Foundation

IFLA (1995) *Seminar on Information Provision to Rural Communities in Africa*, Uppsala University Library: International Federation of Library Associations and Institutions

Kagan, A. (1992) 'Liberation technology', *Progressive Librarian*, 5:47–9

Lancaster, F. W. (1978) *Toward Paperless Information System*, New York: Academic

Levey, L. A. (1991) *Computer and CD-ROM Capability in Sub-Saharan African University and Research Libraries*, Washington: American Association for the Advancement of Science

Levey, L. A. (1992) 'CD-ROM costs and implementation issues', in *CD-ROM for African Research Needs*: 13–22–22

Levey, L. A. (ed) (1993) *A Profile of Research Libraries in Sub-Saharan Africa: Acquisitions, Outreach, and Infrastructure*, Washington: American Association for the Advancement of Science

Maack, M. 'The role of external aid in West African library development', *Library Quarterly*, 56:1–16

Mcharazo, A. A. S. (1985) summary of S. Aruna-chalam's 'Accessing Information Published in the Third World: Should Spreading the Word from the Third World Always be Like Swimming Against the Current?', paper presented to Workshop on Access to Third World Journals, *The African Book Publishing Record*, 20/4:245

Mchombu, K. J. (1982) 'On the librarianship of poverty', *Libri*, 32/3:241–50

Mkandawire, T. (1995) 'Africa's three generations of scholars', *Codesria Bulletin*, 3:1–3

Newa, J. M. (1993) 'The sustainability of information technology innovations — CD-ROM at the University of Dar es Salaam', in H. A. Patrikios and L. A. Levey (eds)

Nyariki, L. and R. Makotsi (1995) 'Problems of book marketing and distribution in Kenya', *African Publishing Review*, 4/2:11

Olden, A. (1987) 'Sub-Saharan African and the paperless society', *Journal of the American Society for Information Science*, 38/4:298–304

Parpart, J. (1995) 'Is Africa a postmodern invention?', *Issue: A Journal of Opinion*, 23/1: 16–18

Patrikios, H. A. (1992) 'Medline in Zimbabwe', in *CD-ROM for African Research Needs*: 30–7–7

Patrikios, H. A. (1993) 'A minimal acquisitions policy for journals at the University of Zimbabwe Medical Library', in Patrikios and Levey (eds)

Patrikios, H. A. and L. A. Levey (eds) (1993) *Survival Strategies in African University Libraries: New Technologies in the Service of Information, Proceedings from a Workshop*, University of Zimbabwe, Harare

Roszak, T. (1993) 'Politics of information and the fate of the Earth', *Progressive Librarian*, 6/7: 3–14

Said, E. (1983) *Culture and Imperialism*. New York: Alfred Knopf

Seeley, J. (1986) 'The use of bibliographic databases in African studies', *African Research and Documentation*, 41:7–12

Sturges, P. and R. Neill (1990) *The Quiet Struggle: Libraries and Information for Africa*, London: Mansell

Tiamiyu, M. A. (1989) 'Sub-Saharan Africa and the paperless society: a comment and a counterpoint', *Journal of the American Society for Information Science*, 40/5:325–8

Zeleza, P. T. (1994) 'Noma Award Acceptance Speech', *The African Book Publishing Record*, 20/4:238

Zeleza, P. T. (forthcoming) 'Trends and inequalities in the production of knowledge on Africa', forthcoming in M. West and W. Martin (eds), *Reconstructing the Study and Meaning of Africa*

Zell, H. M. (1993) 'Publishing in Africa: the crisis and the challenge', in Oyekan Owomoyela (ed), *A History of Twentieth-Century African Literatures*, Lincoln and London: University of Nebraska Press

Zell, H. M. (1995) 'Effective promotion and marketing, and the size of the export market for African books', *African Publishing Review* 4/2:16–18

The author

Paul Tiyambe Zeleza is Professor of History and African Studies and Director of the Center for African Studies of the University of Illinois at Urbana-Champaign. This article was first published in *Development in Practice* Volume 6 Number 4, in 1996.

People's empowerment from the people's perspective[1]

Karunawathie Menike

Why are the poor silent?

The word 'empowerment' is not unfamiliar to us. It implies that we, the Poor, lack power to improve the quality of our lives. It also implies that we lack the necessary strength and capacity to improve our own condition. Numerous programmes are initiated by governments and NGOs in developing countries, to 'empower' the Poor. We do not oppose these. But while we agree they are well intended, we doubt whether they are correctly conceived. When we look at these programmes, we get a feeling that most of them, whether initiated by governments or by NGOs, are based on the false assumption that we, the Poor, do not know how to overcome our poverty and improve our own condition; that we do not have knowledge about the cause of our poverty and how to overcome it; and that we are lethargic and tend to accept our poverty as our fate. It is on this premise that many well-intentioned NGOs and government officials develop their programmes for empowering us. They seem to want to enter our villages to shake us up and wake us from what they think is our slumber and tell us that we must take our future into our own hands to create ways of improving our quality of life.

For us, all this is quite hilarious. Those who plan their 'empowerment' interventions clearly do not understand our reality, our priorities, our wishes, our thought processes, our constraints, and our needs. They do not understand that often the Poor do not take the initiative to empower themselves — not because they don't want to be empowered or because they lack the knowledge and the capacity to do so; or because they don't understand that they can improve their own condition through their own empowerment. If the Poor are silent, it is because they have a deep experiential understanding of their own reality. It is little realised that the Poor not only possess a depth of knowledge about their present social environment, but they also have visions about what they would like to see and towards which they would like to move. But the visions of the Poor are not utopian like those of intellectuals and others who are removed from the earthy realities of life in poor communities.

Our strongest tool is strategy

We are in no hurry to launch upon an accelerated journey to empowerment. We know that in the social, economic, and political conditions in which we are placed, this would be not only unrealistic but self-destructive. The Poor have their own pace and own rhythm of empower-ment: a rhythm that is born out of wisdom and experience and not out of planning on a drawing board, sitting under a fan in a comfortable urban office. The Poor know full well that if they want to empower themselves — which they do — it has to be done very carefully. When doing this in an environment which in every sense is against us, we know full well that our strongest tool is *strategy* — not force and not power. We know that if we try to act fast in a hostile environment, we could easily trip and fall. When a badly strategised empowerment effort fails, as often happens when it is done under pressure for accelerated action, the repercussions are severe. The Poor do not want to fall from the frying pan into the fire, because they cannot afford to do so. What seems to you to be our silence, our reticence, our ignorance, and our lack of purpose is really in fact our strength, our wisdom, and our knowledge.

The Poor certainly know what has to be done and how we should act in order to overcome our poverty and improve our quality of life. Precisely for this reason, we do not want to make the critical moves and act in the way many governments and NGOs want us to act, until the environment matures to the point when such action will bring positive rather than negative results. The Poor know that the processes of development and poverty alleviation are necessarily slow and have to be pursued with care and circumspection. The Poor are not willing to act in a hurry. They are anchored, strongly anchored, in their own experience: the body of knowledge and experience that has sustained them under the most adverse conditions.

The Poor know how government and NGOs in many Southern countries are in a mad hurry to carry out programmes for empowering them. They also know the reasons for that urgency. Politicians are interested in votes. Naturally they are anxious to do something for the Poor, who form the majority of voters. The result of hurried empowerment programmes chasing after short-term results is the creation of a lot of confusion.

Lessons from Sri Lanka

Let me give you one example from my own country, Sri Lanka. The government has started sending hurriedly recruited, rapidly trained paid officers to 'teach the villagers the reasons for their poverty'. In the first place, there is nothing to teach the Poor about the reasons for their poverty, because they know the reasons much better than their Colombo-appointed teachers can explain. Secondly, a government in a hurry recruits officers in a hurry. These officers lack the skill to understand the social environment of our villages or to appreciate the wisdom of the Poor. Instead they act like parrots, preaching to the people what they have memorised from the lecture notes given to them by their trainers. They tell the people that they are poor because the village trader is exploiting them, or because of the bad conduct and lack of commitment of village-level officials. They tell us that we are poor because we don't get from the existing system the resources that are our due. They even take it upon themselves to attack the people's voluntary organisations that have been functioning in our villages for centuries and are a valuable instrument of survival. They tell us that these organisations are corrupt. At the same time, they try to create dreams of instant prosperity and liberation which confuse us unnecessarily. As a result, we find a lot of conflicts developing among the Poor in our villages.

Irresponsible interventions of this kind are not only unnecessary but can also be very harmful. For one thing, what they tell the people is nothing new. We know whether the trader is exploiting us or not. We can judge for ourselves whether the voluntary organisations in our village are corrupt or not. We have the intelligence to judge for ourselves the positive and negative actions of village-level government officials. We do not need a bunch of outsiders to come to our villages and insult our intelligence by assuming that we cannot understand our social environment for ourselves. It is not necessary for outsiders who lack the maturity or the skills to understand the subtleties and realities of rural processes to come to our villages and confuse our people. It is high time that these well-meaning outsiders learned to respect our knowledge, intelligence, and values. For now, the Poor know how to act strategically in their environment to improve their conditions step by step, inch by inch, without antagonising the other elements of rural society, who, if roused by aggressiveness on the part of the Poor, could move fast and make things very much worse.

The Poor have, through centuries of experience, developed an effective system of managing their environment. We plan our strategy very carefully. We do not confront the village trader, because it can be counter-productive to do so. In fact, we become friendly with him, and while on the one hand we get access to his market through our friendship with him, on the other, through our co-operation with him, we get his profits invested in the village itself rather than in the town. We know how to strategise our relationship with the middleman. In our case, the village middlemen never confront us. We have a strategy of collaborating with rather than confronting the other social elements in our village, and strategising the collaboration in such a way that we move towards our own objectives at a slow but easy pace, without antagonising any one, and keeping everyone on good terms with us. This is the management system that is used by the rural poor, strongly influenced by the values and norms that are a part of our heritage. However, it is precisely the norms, the values, and the management systems of the Poor that government programmes and NGOs often tend to destroy through their wrongly conceived interventions and programmes.

Why are NGOs in such a hurry?

So far, I have been speaking of some of the limiting factors in governmental programmes of popular empowerment. Development NGOs also promote many empowerment programmes. They too are in a mighty hurry to implement these and produce instant results. We Poor know why. Most NGOs are linked to foreign donor agencies. Not being financially self-reliant, NGOs enter into contracts regarding the implementation of project proposals. As I know from my own association with NGOs who provide support services for popular organisations such as my own, every project is time-bound. Implementation is limited to one, two, or three years. In my experience, the maximum period is three years. Because of the pressures from the funding agencies with whom they sign contracts, NGOs

are forced to implement their programmes in a hurry and produce instant results to please their donors. In order to show the progress they have made, and qualify for more funding, NGOs have to send regular progress reports. So they have to tell the donor agencies that they have created 50 new jobs, 100 new jobs, and so on. Therefore, irrespective of their feasibility, projects are often imposed on the people by NGOs with foreign donor support.

The Poor are intelligent. Please have no doubt about that. We know that often NGO projects are nothing but conglomerations of activities that are implemented to make somebody abroad happy, or to be able to send beautiful reports to please a donor sitting in a foreign country, blissfully oblivious of the reality on the ground. As for the Poor, when projects that are not really feasible — because they have been planned to fit into the priorities and dreams of urban NGOs and foreign donors — are introduced in their villages, they accept them. They don't reject or oppose them, because, in their poverty, they feel that some little benefit might eventually be derived from them. Poverty is indeed relieved by such projects to a small extent. The resources that come into our villages, even through ill-conceived projects, certainly make our poverty a little more comfortable to endure. But we pay a heavy price for that little comfort. These falsely guided interventions create lots of confusion and problems because they are imposed on, and not planned by, the Poor. The social and economic distortions that result from many such interventions create new problems that the Poor never encountered before. In many villages, instead of empowerment and economic development, economic deterioration, cultural degeneration, and political confusion follow in their wake. The contradictions between the genuine aspirations, pace, and rhythm of the Poor on the one hand and the well-intentioned but ill-conceived programmes implemented 'for' the Poor by governments and NGOs on the other are very important to bear in mind when we talk about 'People's Empowerment'.

There are other more dangerous and serious aspects to some of the interventions that are made in the name of People's Empowerment.

We have experienced that any organisation, whether governmental or NGO, has to sign a bond or agreement with the donors. As a result of these aid contracts, foreigners who have no knowledge about the aspirations or the real conditions of the Poor get the opportunity to realise their own desires and to impose their own values, their own norms, and their own concepts about society on us.

Cultural values must be respected

Let me once again speak from my own personal experience. Let me assume that some foreign country wants ours to be transformed into a playground where people from developed countries can come for enjoyment and pleasure. We, the Poor, have enough experience about what the rich and influential people of our country are like. They keep one foot here and one foot abroad. There are many organisations — including a few NGOs and private business companies — who would not mind helping those foreign countries to convert our motherland into a playground, if this would bring them a few sacks of money. So long as they can get money, they are not bothered about what will happen to the motherland. What prevents this from happening is the barrier represented by our traditional culture, its norms, and its values. In my part of the country, it is the Buddhist culture and the organised Buddhist establishment that has always strongly objected to activities that are destructive of the interests of the Poor. It is the Poor, and not those with one foot in this country and one foot abroad, who have built up and protected this barrier. It is not the economic system or the political culture that prevents the sell-out of our country and our people to foreign interests. It is the cultural barrier, provided in my part of the country by the norms and values of Buddhism, and in other parts of the country by the equally rich traditions and values of Hinduism, Christianity, and Islam, that serves to protect the poor from total domination.

I am sorry to say that in my own experience I have seen many attempts to break these cultural barriers by tempting the Poor with their money.

I am sorry to say that, in the name of development projects, there are several instances where attempts to destroy our culture and our values are taking place in Sri Lanka. Let me relate one of my experiences. One day there was a programme organised for women in our area in the preaching hall of our village temple. All the participants were seated in the preaching hall. A vehicle came and stopped just in front of the entrance and the lecturer walked inside. He did not even bother to look around: straight away he started his lecture. Ours is largely a Buddhist village, and our Buddhist values are strongly opposed to the taking of life. The lecturer taught us about poultry keeping and how we could rear thousands and thousands of chickens and sell them for meat. He taught us how to generate thousands of rupees in 45 days. Next he taught us how to rear fish in the lakes where we bathe, and how we could kill them and sell for the money.

What do these people expect to achieve by encouraging Buddhists to kill animals? Is it only to help us empower ourselves economically? Do they only want to make us rich? Oh my God! don't you understand that they are trying slowly to dominate us with their money, destroy the values that have maintained us for 2,500 years and, by making us effectively non-Buddhists in our villages, break down the cultural barrier that stands in the way of complete domination of our countries by avaricious outsiders? If they think that we do not understand their intentions, let me tell them with all the force that a poor village woman like me can gather, that we understand their intentions very well, but we are too poor and powerless to resist them. I remember how, during the lecture, an old woman commented sarcastically, 'If we can earn so much from rearing chickens, why doesn't the priest do the same, and use the money to construct his own temple? Then we wouldn't need to keep raising funds for the temple by organising fairs.' She murmured this sadly and defiantly. The lecturer did not hear her. Our people know the implications of these programmes, but they don't want to make it public, because they are scared and have no power to oppose. At the same time, because of their poverty, quite a few people are attracted by such programmes and do participate in them. Please do not misunderstand me. I am not trying to say that it is only Buddhist values that are being destroyed. From what I know, these same forces are also destroying Hindu values in Hindu villages, Christian values in Christian villages, and Islamic values in Islamic villages: it is a process that tries to destroy the cultural roots of the Poor — be they Buddhists, Hindus, Christians, or Muslims.

What is the final outcome of these manoeuvres which are perpetrated in the name of People's Empowerment? The people's culture is destroyed, and with it the roots and the anchorage of the Poor. The power of the people deteriorates and in its wake follows economic and social deterioration. We get thrown into further dependency on foreign countries, and our power is further weakened. Our humane system of managing our social and political environment gets replaced by the inhumane, technical, materialistic management system of the North. Our culture teaches us that we should not destroy and punish those who have done wrong. Our own values teach us how we can reform a person who has done wrong and bring him or her back to the mainstream of society, and how such a person can re-integrate with society and come back to a more balanced pattern of life. But see what is happening to the values of our communities because of the small-scale savings and credit schemes that are being introduced, through governmental programmes and NGO initiatives. What do the organisations and agencies that provide the capital for these schemes insist should be done in the case of loan defaulters? 'Isolate the man or woman,' they say. 'Don't associate with him or her; use social pressure: ostracise the defaulter. Get the money back somehow.' So with one hand they give us aid, and with the other hand they impose values which are destructive of our own principles — values which in my view are evil and unacceptable. In the name of Aid, in the name of Empowerment, we become culturally disempowered. What a destruction. What a price we pay for Aid. And remember, it is all done in the name of People's Empowerment.

Empowering the poor means trusting the poor

I repeat, I am not for a moment saying that all NGO and government programmes that are implemented for People's Empowerment are counter-productive and disempowering. What I do maintain is that the majority of such programmes are well intended but badly conceived. What I am trying to say on behalf of the Poor is that many government officials and NGO leaders do not see reality from our angle. My plea is that you should make a real effort to put yourself in our position, in the position of the Poor, and look at the reality as we see it. I appeal to you that, in the programmes that you plan, you should leave no room for the destruction of our traditional cultures and our traditional values, in the name of People's Empowerment. We, the Poor, do not have much decision-making power or strength within the overall order of things. We have a little power, which we maximise through the application of our wisdom and through the careful planning of our own strategies of empowerment. *I appeal to you — do not do anything, even with the best of intentions, that will destroy the little power and strength we possess.* If you want to empower the Poor, please first trust the Poor. The People can teach you — and not the other way round. Please do not come to teach the Poor and impose your values and strategies on us because of your false notion that the Poor are ignorant, lethargic, and need to be shaken up. Don't insult the Poor. Allow the People's Movements to take their own decisions, and to plan and manage their resources. Let them seek solutions to their own problems.

I do not say that the Popular Organisations and Popular Movements do not need or want the help and co-operation of NGOs. We need your support. But let *us* decide and *you* support us. We are not ready to let you decide for us — we have not mandated you to do so. We need your support for implementing our own decisions. You may support us in technology, in marketing, in accessing resources, in building our institutions, in solving a problem, or in helping us understand the workings of the wider world. But instead of imposing your decisions on us, which unfortunately you tend to do, give the power to the Poor, so that we may decide through our own organisation when and how to obtain the support we want, both from NGOs and from the government. Support us — but don't direct us. We would like to direct you, because we are the Poor and you are our supporters. Give the power to the Poor to choose the kind of development they want and to choose their support services for themselves. If resources are directly transferred to Popular Organisations instead of through NGOs, the people will be empowered to decide what support services they require, and from what NGOs and agencies they should obtain them.

I would like to see the day when NGOs will have to provide the services that the people want, and not the services that the donors and other agencies choose to deliver to the people. NGOs, whose support we will always want, will then become more efficient and effective, because they will have to compete with each other to provide what the people require and for which the people will have the resources to pay. There will be competition among NGOs to provide these services. They will then try to do their best. Then, and then alone, will there be real change. Then it can be said more truthfully that the people have been empowered. People will then get the power to maintain their self-respect and, if necessary, to reject those foreign donor agencies who do not want to support the decisions of the Poor or the proposals of NGOs who are responding to them. The Poor do not want you to impose your programmes to empower us. We know how to empower ourselves. We want your support for our decisions.

In conclusion, it is my duty to say something about our host — IRED.[2] I am grateful to IRED on behalf of the rural poor — and especially on behalf of the rural women — for giving us an opportunity to participate in an international colloquy. There are always conferences to talk about us, the Poor. But almost never are we, the Poor, given an opportunity to participate in them. We are told that we don't know English, don't know how to use the big words that are used at these conferences, don't understand all the nonsense that is being spoken in our name,

and that we therefore cannot be allowed to participate. In my experience as a peasant woman, IRED has always taken a different position on these matters. Our peasant organisations have associated with IRED since 1986. IRED has always given pride of place to the people, their values, their norms, their cultures, and their way of doing things. In all the IRED meetings that I have attended in Sri Lanka, they have provided a place of honour for our national languages, Sinhala and Tamil, and provided a platform for the Poor to articulate their priorities, aspirations, needs, and problems.

Notes

1 This is an adapted extract from the keynote speech delivered by Mrs Menike at the Asian Regional Colloquy held in Colombo, Sri Lanka, in July 1992, entitled 'People's Empowerment in Asia — Myth or Reality', organised by IRED. The full speech is published by IRED's Development Support Services (DSS): Asia, as an Occasional Paper entitled 'People's Empowerment as the People See It'.

2 IRED (Development Innovations and Networks), based in Geneva, facilitates exchanges of experience among grassroots organisations, promotes the development of new networks and group federations, and provides technical support in a wide range of organisational and technical skills.

The author

Karunawathie Menike is a peasant leader from Wilpotha in north-west Sri Lanka. At the time of writing, she was Chairperson of the People's Rural Development Association (PRDA), which brings together the business, scientific, and professional communities of Sri Lanka, as well as development NGOs and community-based organisations, to promote employment and income generation through small-enterprise development in the rural sector. This article first appeared in *Development in Practice* Vol 3 Number 3 in 1993.

Building partnerships between Northern and Southern NGOs

Alan Fowler

Introduction

All development decades have their emphases. The 1980s were dominated by an economic ideology of adjustment, coupled with an institutional doctrine promoting private enterprise and encouraging non-government organisations (NGOs).[1] The stress on privatising development has led to sharp increases in official aid to NGOs, giving rise to a rapid growth in their numbers worldwide, as well as provoking new debates about the desired relationship and division of labour between NGOs in the North and South.[2] A common conclusion of these dialogues is that 'partnerships' have to be created between them. Unfortunately, the term 'partnership' is so ill-defined and so over-used that it is in danger of losing a serviceable meaning.

Rather than elaborate on the content of NGO partnerships, as has been done by others, this article tries to further the discussion in two ways. Firstly, it responds to a frequent complaint of many NGO leaders that they are disadvantaged when negotiating with Northern NGOs about partnership, because they know less about Northern counterparts than the counterparts know about them. 'Not transparent' is an expression often used by Southern NGO leaders to describe their perception of Northern NGOs. The primary concern of this article, therefore, is to counter such an imbalance by providing a general review of Northern NGOs, their origins, growth, and contexts. Secondly, by drawing on experiences mainly from eastern and southern Africa, issues are identified that are likely to influence the negotiation of NGO partnerships in the 1990s. In concluding, the search for partnership is placed within the context of current thinking about the 'third' or 'value-driven' sector in society.

Northern NGOs

History and growth in numbers

The tradition of private foreign aid dates back to the mid-seventeenth century; the involvement of secular voluntary agencies in development began in the mid-nineteenth century. While often linked to missionary activity, European NGOs did not, even then, restrict themselves only to the 'good works' of charity and welfare. Lobbying governments and other advocacy work of NGOs is not just a recent affair; for example, it is to be found in their opposition and rallying against the slave trade. Broadly speaking, however, the emergence of Northern NGOs specifically interested in development of the Third World has religious roots and is a phenomenon of the last 50 years. (Oxfam, for example, was founded in 1942 and CARE in 1945.)

The role of Northern NGOs in Third World development has grown steadily. From being obscure, peripheral development actors in the 1950s, 1960s, and much of the 1970s, NGOs moved to the centre of the stage in the 1980s. Available (but not altogether reliable) figures[3] suggest that the total number of development NGOs in the North (OECD countries) in 1987 was in the order of 2,540, up from 350 in 1900. In 1981, an estimated 1,700 NGOs (excluding the denominational church-based development organisations) were involved in Third World development, indicating a growth of 50 per cent in nine years. The current total of Northern NGOs includes the following:

- about 1,400 in Western Europe;
- approximately 190 in Japan;
- about 700 in the USA;
- some 250 in Canada (up from 67 in 1968/69, with 16 per cent of all Canadian development NGOs being founded in the five-year period 1980–85).

The growth of Northern NGOs is likewise reflected in their presence in the South. For example, foreign NGOs registered in Kenya increased by 260 per cent in the period 1977–78. Indigenous NGOs increased by 156 per cent in the same period.

Growth in resources

The increase in Northern NGOs has been more than matched by the growth in the financial resources they use to support development in the South. However, Northern NGOs are raising less money themselves, and are channelling more from the official development assistance (ODA) of governments, as the following figures[4] indicate:

- The funds raised by NGOs *from the public* for Third World relief and development rose from US$1.3 billion in 1975 to US$4.2 billion in 1988 (the rate of growth of the increase in *public* donations was almost twice as high in other OECD countries as in the USA).[5]

- The funds from ODA channelled to NGOs for development increased to US$2.3 billion in 1988, an increase of 310 per cent since 1975. This amounts to 4.6 per cent of total ODA. Nowadays, 34 per cent of the total funds used by Northern NGOs comes from official sources.

- The growth of NGO income from official sources has been much higher than that from the general public.

- The value of the total resources transferred from NGOs to the Third World accounts for about 15 per cent of total overseas development assistance.

- In 1984, 59 per cent of Canadian NGOs obtained more than half of their funds from the Canadian government, compared with 48 per cent of NGOs in 1980. By comparison, in 1982, only 14 per cent of Dutch NGOs obtained more than half of their funds from government sources.

- Many multilateral agencies, such as the World Bank, International Labour Organization (ILO), United Nations Development Programme (UNDP), and the Food and Agriculture Organization (FAO), have developed special funds for and relationships with NGOs. In fact all official agencies now appear to have an 'open door' policy towards NGOs.

- The amount of *direct funding* from official donors to *Southern* NGOs is (conservatively) estimated to have risen from US$10.5 million in 1980 to US$37 million in 1983, and to have grown even more strongly since then.

These figures show two distinct trends. First, the dependence of the NGO development sector on ODA is undergoing a phenomenal increase, far above the economic growth rates of their countries. Second, more and more NGOs are in danger of becoming quasi-governmental, as the proportion of official funding they enjoy overtakes that from private donors. A direct implication for Southern NGOs in any partnership discussion in the 1990s is that they should ascertain the actual sources of Northern NGOs' funds. For without such insight it will be difficult to assess what a potential partner can or cannot negotiate about, and the degree of control which they may or may not have over decisions.

Northern NGOs in context

Any generalisations about the origins and characteristics of Northern NGOs and the environment in which they operate will not do justice to any one NGO or country. But not to generalise would be even less helpful to Southern NGOs trying to understand the NGO sector in the North. As Chambers says, 'with today's centralization of power and communications ... we have to generalize: not to do so is to generalize by default. The problem is how to do it better.'[6]

Origins: the sources of diversity

Northern NGOs are as diverse as the contexts in which they have grown: they cannot be easily labelled by type. The first important point to be made, therefore, is that they are *heterogeneous*: no two are the same, and all strive to maintain their individual identities. In fact, promoting identity is an important component in negotiating partnerships — a point we will return to later.

The origins of Northern NGOs and the constituencies they relate to are diverse and often complex. Following are some of the factors that have influenced the formation, character, and agendas of Northern NGOs.

Political affiliations

Some NGOs trace their roots directly to a political party or movement in their country. Examples are the German *Stiftungs* (Foundations) named after various German political party leaders, such as Friedrich Ebert, Konrad Adenauer, and Hans Seidel. Norwegian People's Aid is closely affiliated to the Norwegian Labour Party. These 'political' NGOs represent the thinking and interests of particular socio-economic groupings. Their political origins and on-going influence virtually guarantee them long-term funding from the central government, irrespective of the party in power. Such NGOs can also maintain substantial autonomy from the government of the day.

Social, cultural, and religious structures

A feature similar but not identical to the above is the class of NGOs which reflect major social structures within a country. An example are the four co-financing NGOs of the Netherlands which reflect the *verzuiling* (denominational

divisions) of Dutch society. Very many facets of Dutch civil and political life are divided along Protestant, Catholic, and secular lines. This is the case with schools, trade unions, television, and radio broadcasting. The consequent division of political parties along such lines allows a natural affinity between these parties and the four co-financing NGOs: CEBEMO (Catholic), ICCO (Protestant), NOVIB (secular), and HIVOS (humanist). The security of funding and autonomy noted above for the political affiliates are also usually enjoyed by these NGOs.

A concern to promote (national) values

Most, if not all, Western societies are concerned to promote the basic values which have enabled them to overcome mass poverty and evolve as representative democracies. Therefore, NGOs are funded to further these values — broadly translated into improving human well-being — all over the world, with some pursuing specific concerns such as human rights, justice, and the rule of law. Examples are Oxfam, various child-sponsorship agencies, Amnesty International, Africa Watch, Asia Watch, and the Anti-Slavery Society. Moreover, all Northern NGOs tend to reflect and are expected to express and advance the values of the (segment of) society from which they have grown.

Ideological identification

Some Northern NGOs find their roots in a particular ideological imperative, often derived from a specific social analysis. Examples are groups set up to support Tanzania's *Ujamaa* experiment, or to show solidarity with the freedom struggle in Zimbabwe and Mozambique; and action groups working against apartheid through boycotts of South African produce.

Issues

NGOs can arise from special issues which confront the North, but then develop a concern for the same issue in the South. Examples are NGOs concerned with environmental pollution and protection, women and gender, abortion, and access to information. Issues that stimulate the creation of a Northern NGO can also emanate from the South. Recent Southern crises of hunger, drought, and famine in the Sahel region of Africa have spawned a number of new Northern NGOs. BandAid/LiveAid was formed to help to alleviate the consequences of the Ethiopian famine. The Hunger Project in the USA was set up to draw attention to the whole question of African agriculture and food security. Obviously communication and the media can play a large role in determining what constitutes a Southern 'issue'. This can be open to manipulation by groups wishing to gain from the plight of others.

Personal identifications and institutional similarities

Occasionally, Northern NGOs are formed as a result of the personal identification of individuals in the North with a specific group or situation in the South, or with institutions that have inherent similarities. Examples are the 'adoption' or twinning of a school in the South with a school in the North because of an expatriate who has worked in both. Northern NGOs may be set up to become involved in Third World development because they have an institutional partner in the South. Religious NGOs — Christian and Islamic — are created on the basis of their obvious (historical) relations with Southern religious groups. Boy Scouts and Girl Guides, trade unions, Rotary Clubs, and professional bodies may also become partners in development, although they may not create a special organisation to do so. The South–North 'twinning' of towns and cities is another example of NGO initiative springing from institutional similarity and identification.

The market

NGOs can also emerge as a response to an increasing availability of resources and capacity to lobby. This is clearly the case in North America. Because two sets of inter-related dynamics stimulated NGO growth in the 1980s, it is difficult to separate cause and effect. In the last decade, ruling political parties in the West have adopted privatisation policies, aimed at reducing the role of government in the economy and public life. However, NGOs have long been lobbying for increased government support for their sector, arguing that they are better placed to promote sustainable development for the poor. The confluence of political ideology and NGO pressure has now dramatically increased the resources available to NGOs. The increased availability of official aid has stimulated a surge in the registration of new NGOs, and increased their dependence on it. Hence, many NGOs are a product of the space and resources newly available to them. The type of NGO produced by this situation can be described as responsive or opportunistic, depending on your viewpoint.

Constituency

One of the more difficult questions to answer for Northern (and Southern) NGOs is: from which constituency in society does an NGO derive its legitimacy? By what mandate does a development NGO have a right to set itself up? The answers to these questions are sometimes clear, but often they are not, and this leaves room for abuse. NGOs created in response to easier accessibility of official funding seldom have a constituency at all. They are effectively owned by individuals, but choose non-profit legal status in order to gain easier access to funding. It is difficult to envisage what a partnership with these NGOs may entail, beyond a mutual interest in gaining access to money.

Tracing the roots of an NGO should clarify the constituency issue, but all too frequently results in a questioning of the personal motivations of an NGO's founders and staff. The problem of how Northern NGOs derive legitimacy for their existence from the poor in the Third World, who are often their *raison d'être*, is thorny but increasingly relevant. Crudely put, the more definite the constituency of an NGO — in terms of an identifiable Northern public and their funding — the higher its legitimacy is likely to be, as its mandate is tied to support from and accountability to the public at large.

Purpose

All NGOs involved in Third World relief and development will probably have stated publicly that their overall purpose is the improvement of the lives and situations of the (poorer) people of the Third World. Some NGOs go on to define themselves by specifying the following:

- a particular set of *intended beneficiaries* of their efforts: disabled people, the poorest of the poor, women, children, single parents, pregnant teenagers, religious groups, trade unionists, co-operatives, refugees, the marginalised, entre-preneurs, etc.;

- particular *problem(s) to be addressed*: world-wide and localised inequity; access to water, health care, education, family planning, credit; sustainable agriculture; appropriate technology; environmental degradation; communication; policy analysis, etc.

Method

The methods used by Northern NGOs to attain their purposes can be

- *direct*, by undertaking development activities themselves in the South (for example, PLAN, CARE, and ActionAid); or

- *indirect*: in the South by assisting existing local organisations (for example NOVIB, ICCO, Christian Aid, Oxfam, World Educa-tion); in the North by development education activities, lobbying, and analytical studies (for example, the World Development Movement in Britain and the Development Group for Alternative Policies (D-GAP) in the USA).

Frequently, Northern NGOs use more than one of these methods. NGOs that raise money from the public almost always adopt development education as one of their fund-raising tools. Others, who operate directly in the South, can use the experience and information they gain to fund-raise from the public and to lobby government. In other words, Northern NGOs often take on a set of (ideally) mutually reinforcing methods to attain their purpose(s).

Identifying the mix

Any Southern NGO which contemplates accepting assistance from a Northern NGO, whether there is the prospect of a partnership or not, is advised to draw up an organisational profile of its counterpart. This means ascer-taining two things: first, the origins, history, and constituency of the Northern NGO (this could be

done using the above points as a guide); secondly, the Southern NGO must determine exactly where the Northern NGO's resources come from and under what conditions. These insights are a prerequisite for any move towards negotiating a partnership. From this knowledge base, the items noted in subsequent sections of this article should be taken into consideration as discussions progress.

Negotiating partnerships with Northern NGOs

The quest for NGO partnerships during the last five to ten years has already revealed a number of difficulties that can arise in the process. In all probability these problems will grow in the 1990s as the NGO sector continues to expand and its role *vis à vis* the State becomes both clearer and more contested. But, equally important, the way that partnerships are sought, negotiated, and formed will affect the nature of Southern NGOs in their own development arena. It is therefore critical that Southern NGOs comprehend the grounds on which Northern NGOs choose to pursue partnerships, and the crucial issues that arise in negotiation. Follow-ing are some of them.

Natural partners: rationale, territory, and maintenance of identity

The concept of a *natural partner* is important to understand if one wants to analyse the behaviour of many Northern NGOs. The concept tries to capture the inclination of a Northern NGO to identify an 'ideal' Southern NGO to collaborate with. Northern NGOs usually view a Southern NGO as a natural partner if the Southern NGO has origins, interests, values, intended bene-ficiaries, constituencies, and objectives similar to those of the Northern NGO itself. Progressive NGOs seek progressive partners, sectorally specialised NGOs seek similar bodies, and so it goes on. The underlying assumption is that such natural partners will 'speak the same language' as the Northern NGO, so making work more productive and efficient. The unspoken premise is, however, that the Southern NGO mirrors the Northern agency. The reverse is seldom expected or accepted.

Natural partners can lead to natural territorialism. For example, for secular NOVIB to fund a Protestant church's development efforts in Africa might tread on the toes of ICCO (Inter-Church Coordination Committee for Development Projects), as ICCO considers Protestant churches to be *its* natural partners. Further, a particular type of Southern NGO can furnish a 'territory' which an NGO feels is natural for it to 'claim'. This is most apparent with the geographic divisions and competition between Protestant churches. In a wider sense, some arguments used in support of the generally negative response of Northern NGOs to official aid agencies' current desire to fund Southern NGOs directly are derived from a belief in natural partners, i.e. that Northern governments are not the natural, and therefore appropriate, partners of Southern NGOs.

An additional consequence of 'natural partner' behaviour is that Northern NGOs with similar cultures and values will end up (competitively) funding the same NGO. It is not unusual in Zimbabwe, for example, to find that Oxfam (UK and Ireland), Oxfam (Canada), NOVIB and HIVOS of the Netherlands, Canadian University Service Overseas (CUSO), British War on Want, and FOS of Belgium are all supporting the same Southern NGO, especially if there is a limited supply of 'suitable' NGOs in a country.

Collaborating with natural partners helps to confirm the identity of Northern NGOs through a process of like-minded reinforcement. Natural partners contribute to a justification of the NGO's presence and activities. If a Northern NGO can demonstrate that there are similar Southern organisations, it implies that the organisation has legitimacy beyond its own origins. The existence of natural partners strengthens the rationale and legitimacy of a Northern NGO's involvement in development.

A distinct advantage of the 'natural partner' concept is that it can be one way of improving mutual understanding. This could be done by each NGO describing what it considers to be its ideal partner, and explaining why. Analysing such descriptions could help to illuminate factors which have contributed to the origins and values of both NGOs — a necessary condition for a partnership. Identifying natural partners remains an important tool and part of the agenda for NGO partnerships in the 1990s.

Not all relationships are partnerships

Partnerships are one type of relationship. The distinctive feature of a partnership is that it involves sharing, with a sense of mutuality and equality between the parties. Both sides of the partnership equation are of equal value — although not necessarily of the same content. How can partnerships be created out of relationships when the parties involved differ so much in their roots, contexts, and resources?

There is no medicine or treatment that, when prescribed, will turn a relationship into a partnership. However, past practice suggests that some conditions have to be fulfilled before Southern and Northern NGOs can truly say that their relationship has made a qualitative change to a partnership. Together with others discussed above, the following conditions need to be satisfied.

A mutually understood 'product'

The items placed on each side of the scales in a South–North partnership are not identical, so it is very important that their individual values are weighed and correctly assessed. For example, how much do the grassroots contacts of Southern NGOs weigh against the technologies and information that a Northern NGO can offer? The only way that these and other questions can be answered in order to make up the balance and provide a sense of equality in relationships is when the 'product' of the joint efforts is mutually agreed. For example, if one NGO collaborating on improving water availability sees the product of water development as a statistically measurable increase in people's access to improved water sources, while the other sees it as increasing a community's capacity to manage its resources, there may be too little common ground on which to agree on the value of what each is bringing into the relationship.

The more we know about development, the more we see that it is both a set of outcomes — impacts which improve people's lives — and a set of processes by which people achieve the outcomes in appropriate and sustainable ways. A detailed understanding and agreement is needed between both parties on what development entails. In other words, NGO dialogue must move beyond projects to a more fundamental exchange on the causes of poverty and the nature of its alleviation.[7]

Such a discussion is also needed about the development of Southern NGOs themselves. For, if development in society is now also understood to include the presence of strong and competent Southern NGOs, we need to agree on what this means and how it can be achieved. Too often, the roots, environments, and institutional self-interests of NGOs precondition them to have different ideas about the products of development and the path to its attainment. Differences need to be expressed and a common ground arrived at, for only then can the value of what each has to offer be properly weighed.

Trust

Another condition for partnership is trust between the parties. Attaining a sufficient degree of trust requires time and a great deal of transparency between organisations. Transparency is normally present if NGOs know of each other's roots, constituency, methods of gaining legitimacy, systems for maintaining accountability, ways in which power is divided in the organisation, and methods of making decisions. It also requires an accord on how conditions accepted by one party which may affect the other (say to receive government money) are discussed and agreed upon. Further, agreements are needed on the image which each party projects of its partner in its own environments, through fund-raising, reporting, etc. Finally, there has to be a realistic and honest appraisal of each other's strengths and weaknesses.

The forgotten element: development legitimacy

The issue of legitimacy is gaining attention because of the rapid expansion of NGOs and the greater volume of public funds involved in their work. Legitimacy is also a critical component in turning NGO relationships into partnerships. Having skills and resources to transfer to the South does not, in itself, make a Northern development NGO legitimate. And it is here that Southern NGOs have a special weight to put in the partnership scales, for they provide the legitimacy for Northern NGOs that support them. Put simply, a unique contribution which Southern NGOs can make to the partnership balance is the provision of legitimacy for Northern development NGOs.

The ultimate legitimacy of development NGOs, Southern and Northern, can be derived only from what they achieve in their relationship with the intended beneficiaries of their existence and efforts: the poor. Southern NGOs can obtain this legitimacy directly in the Third World; most Northern NGOs that are not operational can obtain it only via their partnerships. This places a critical obligation on Southern NGOs to be legitimate themselves. Recognition of this factor provides the grounds for the mutual dependency that should characterise a true partnership. Such a view implies a necessary qualitative shift from the present relationship pattern, whereby Southern NGOs are treated as a dependent part of a development-delivery system for Northern resources and knowledge.

The question of legitimacy of NGOs, North and South, will be asked more and more in the years to come as their numbers increase, as more studies are carried out on their performance, as more diverse relationships are developed between NGOs and other types of organisation, and as the resources used by NGOs become increasingly 'official'. Development NGOs need to be aware that their origins and motives will be subject to more analysis and discussion. They will have to answer some searching inquiries, and statements of personal motivation and commitment will not suffice.

Partnership as projection

The pursuit of natural partnership described above can go one step too far. For it is not uncommon to see Northern NGOs 'projecting' or forcing on to the partner the image that the Northern NGO wants to see. This is usually done through initial partner selection, demanding particular styles or types of leadership and management, forcing priorities and methods, attaching conditions to funds, requiring individualised reporting formats, and so on. Such an image often reflects an idealised vision which the Northern NGO has of itself. How often do Northern NGOs want partner organisations to be self-sufficient, democratic, reliable, efficient, progressive, gender-balanced, and whatever else is part of the self-image that the Northern NGO cannot itself attain? If one analysed the gender structures or internal democracy or efficiency of a Northern NGO, one would seldom find a much better picture than in those they support. In the case of the Kenya Freedom From Hunger Council (KFFHC), for example, one donor (out of four) became so frustrated at the inability of the Council to reflect its own image by doing things exactly the way it wanted (the four donors could not reach a compromise together) that it resorted to actually *running its own projects* within KFFHC, managed by its own staff, using its own reporting formats — and yet this donor still refers to the relationship as a partnership!

Southern NGOs are usually aware of the tendency of Northern NGOs to project themselves on to the partner. They need to guard against it by ensuring that they have a strong identity as a foundation for their negotiating position. For, without a firm sense of self, Southern NGOs are liable to mirror Northern NGOs by default.

One-way mirrors

Negotiations about partnership have clearly highlighted the confusion and mistrust that can arise when a Northern donor NGO does not indicate where its funds are coming from. The Organisation of Rural Associations for Progress in Zimbabwe (ORAP) initiated the creation of a consortium among its long-term donors in order to overcome the many problems of multi-sourced multiple-project funding. Through the interaction it became apparent that, while each

donor presented a different individual image in its approach to ORAP, with strong tones of solidarity and identification, when it came to requirements of reporting, their demands were stringent and very similar. Why? Because for many donors the sources of their funds were governments that tend to have uniform, tight standards that are applied world-wide, irrespective of the recipient. The needs of ORAP were difficult to accommodate. Communication in one direction — towards ORAP — manifested solidarity, but in the other direction — requirements from ORAP — revealed mistrust. A lack of transparency in funding sources resulted in what can be typified as a one-way-mirror relationship. Northern NGOs must therefore be open about the conditions they have accepted on behalf of those whom they support.

The limits to partnership

The pursuit of NGO partnerships began with an ambitious and confusing start in the 1980s, because the concept was simultaneously treated as (a) an ideological statement that would demonstrate the strength of a Northern NGO's commitment to solidarity in the development cause, and (b) as a set of new collaborative mechanisms and funding practices. The various attempts at relational innovation tried out over the last ten years, such as programme funding, delegation of responsibilities to partners, local partner 'platforms', reverse consortia, and organisational decentralisation, can all be seen dualistically as an ideological positioning along the progressive–conservative NGO continuum, and also as practical attempts to change the expressions of power within what is an inherently unbalanced relationship. It is not surprising, therefore, that partnership has often been idealised, and efforts to construct it competitive.

What is apparent from experience is, first, that partnership can have two distinct levels: partnerships between the individuals who work in Southern and Northern NGOs, and partnerships between NGOs as institutions. While individuals can adopt partnership-type behaviours, the difficulty of creating institutional partnerships for Northern NGOs is that they have to be able to adapt to a multiplicity of Southern NGOs, and this is organisationally difficult to achieve. The imbalance in funder–recipient relations puts the onus of adaptation on the Southern NGO. As a consequence, the management of multiple partners is a major headache for many of them, a fact that partnership should in fact help to rectify. Second, partnership is not a blanket covering all aspects of a relationship, for successful partnerships frequently depend on the prevailing ethos, and the issues and people involved.[8] Third, a distinction needs continually to be drawn between responsibility and authority. Responsibilities can be shared in a partnership; authority seldom can. If this is not clear from the outset, mutually false expectations can be created.

The 1990s are likely to see a decrease in the flexibility of Northern NGOs, as they become increasingly dependent on official aid as their source of funds. This would suggest that from the outset each party should define precisely (a) what they want a partnership for, and (b) what organisational adaptation is possible, and on offer, and what is not negotiable. For example, partnership could be sought in the sharing of information and strategies for action in the South, and coupling them to advocacy in the North, as has been successfully done on environmental issues without any funding; or agreements could be made on reciprocating human-resource development and training opportunities in both NGOs. Or planning cycles could be timed to coincide; or a rolling funding system could be agreed, in order to reduce cash-flow management problems; or an agreement made to schedule visitors for specific periods in the year. In sum, building partnerships in the 1990s should be more specific, nuanced, and pragmatic, rather than the all-embracing, excessively ideological approach to building NGO relations that has characterised earlier years.

Summary

This article has offered pointers for Southern and Northern NGOs wishing to improve their partnership negotiations. It has stressed the need for mutual openness and transparency, with a bias towards providing Southern NGOs with information and categories by which they can better understand their Northern counterparts. It has been suggested that building partnerships would be improved by (a) creating a partner profile in terms of origins, affiliations, constituency, purpose; (b) describing the natural partner; (c) determining original funding sources; (d) stating positions on the processes and products of development; (e) clarifying legitimacy; (f) avoiding projection and one-way mirrors; and (g) being specific about the areas in which partnership is sought and is possible. No method can guarantee the creation of effective partnerships, but, as the foregoing are drawn from experiences to date, such an approach should contribute to progress in the years to come.

NGOs in the third sector

Increasingly, NGOs are being seen as one type of institution in the 'third sector' of society. The organisations in this sector differentiate themselves from governments and commercial enterprise in that their purposes are driven by values, whereas the primary objectives of governments are to control and regulate, and those of businesses are to make profits for the owners. As we move towards the twenty-first century, NGOs are being called upon to take on a greater role in global development. Governments are seen to be inefficient and (often) corrupt, and commercial enterprise too self-serving and concerned with short-term gain to provide hope for sustainable livelihoods for the world's population. Success in taking up this challenge will depend on the emergence of a strong third sector within society. The power of NGOs in the third — value-driven — sector will depend to an important degree on their ability to form coalitions across ethnic, class, spiritual, geographical, and national boundaries.

NGO partnerships are one link in a system of civic affiliations that urgently need to be forged in this decade in order to increase our hope for more equitable and sustainable development in the next century. Viewing partnerships as one part of a broader strategy in the development of the value-driven sector of society may help to persuade NGOs to temper self-interest in their negotiations, in order to achieve fundamental realignments in society for the common good.

Notes

1 The term 'development NGO' usually includes membership organisations such as village groups and community development associations created to support the development of the poor in Third World countries. However, this article restricts itself to non-membership NGOs.

2 'The North' consists of member countries in the Organisation of Economic Cooperation and Development (OECD); 'official aid' is the finance allocated to development by the member governments. 'The South' refers to countries receiving official aid.

3 These data are derived from calculations using the following sources: Lissner: *The Politics of Altruism: A Study of the Political Behaviour of Voluntary Agencies* (Geneva: Lutheran World Federation, 1977); L. Bolling and C. Smith: *Private Foreign Aid* (Boulder: Westview Press, 1982); OECD: *Voluntary Aid in Development: The Role of Non-Governmental Organisations* (Paris, 1988); C. Stevens and C. van Thermaat: *Pressure Groups, Policies, and Development* (London: Hodder and Stoughton, 1985); InterAction: *Diversity in Development* (Washington); T. Brodhead and B. Herbert-Copley: *Bridges of Hope?* (Ottawa: The North-South Institute, 1988); Canadian Council for International Development: 'Mind If I Cut In?' (Ottawa, mimeo, 1988); OECD: *Directory of Non-Governmental Development Organisations in OECD Member Countries* (Paris, 1990); JANIC: *Directory of Non-Governmental Organisations in Japan: NGOs Active in International Cooperation* (Tokyo: Japan Center for International Cooperation, 1990).

4 Sources as in note (3).

5 In relation to 1987 equivalent values, the amount for 1977–79 is US$2.87 billion, against US$3.94 billion in 1988 — an increase in real terms of 40 per cent.

6 R. Chambers: *The State and Rural Development: Ideologies and an Agenda for the 1990s* (Discussion Paper No. 269, Institute of Development Studies, University of Sussex).

7 The choice of development processes and products should derive from some analysis and theory about poverty. But, as Tim Brodhead, President of the Canadian Council for International Cooperation, points out, many development NGOs in North America have no theory of (under)development to inform or underpin their actions. He considers the articulation of a theory of development to be a *sine qua non* for the legitimacy of any NGO working in this field. (Personal communication.)

8 This section draws on conversations with Sithembiso Nyone of ORAP, Zimbabwe.

The author

Alan Fowler has been working with NGOs for some twenty years as manager, consultant, donor, writer, and researcher, and as a Visiting Fellow at the World Bank and the Society for Participatory Research in Asia. In 1991 he co-founded the International NGO Training and Research Centre (INTRAC). He is currently an independent consultant based in the Philippines. This article was first published in *Development in Practice* Volume 1, Number 1 (1991).

The evaporation of gender policies in the patriarchal cooking pot[1]

Sara Hlupekile Longwe

The basic problem is this: the 1985 Nairobi World Conference on Women set out ambitious goals and strategies, but since then little or no progress has been made. Ten years later in Beijing, we had to admit that the level of women's representation in national politics has not improved, and there is an increased feminisation of poverty. In many Islamic countries, the decade has seen increasing gender discrimination and oppression.

This lack of progress is despite the fact that the policies of development agencies have been considerably changed by the *Nairobi Forward-Looking Strategies*. By the early 1990s, almost every agency had improved its stated goals and strategies, incorporating intentions to contribute to the process of women's empowerment. Most agencies have also adopted policies of 'gender mainstreaming', to address gender issues in all projects and programmes.

How does the Beijing *Platform for Action* respond to the lack of progress since 1985? The response has not been a re-consideration of the goals and strategies defined in Nairobi. Rather, the *Platform* sets out a more detailed plan to achieve these same goals. Firstly, it demands more specific commitments from governments; secondly, it sets out in more detail the ways to achieve these commitments; and thirdly, it proposes improved international machinery for monitoring and evaluating progress. In short, the formula is more of the same.

The *Platform* is written as if we are all pulling together in tackling common problems. It is underpinned by an implicit assumption of good will, as if the international push for women's advancement were like the eradication of polio — which nobody opposes, and no government is likely to subvert.

If the assumptions underlying this apparent consensus were to be made explicit, how many of us would consider such assumptions to be appropriate or realistic? What is lacking in such discourse is any admission of the extent to which women's advancement faces patriarchal opposition. The consensus discourse conceals the essence of the problem. We are up against a hidden agenda of patriarchal opposition which needs to be seen, understood, and analysed, as the prerequisite for progress.

Gender policies have a strange tendency to 'evaporate' within international development agencies. Are we going to recognise and discuss this, or pretend the problem isn't there? Are we still to treat it as a 'hidden' problem? Surely, it is obvious enough to any feminist who has ever tried to work with one of these agencies.

This article looks into this problem, which lies hidden within the official vocabulary, but is otherwise clear. We shall consider the case of the development agency as a 'patriarchal cooking pot' in which gender policies evaporate. We shall explore this process of policy evaporation: why it happens, and how it happens. This 'patriarchal pot' is not introduced merely for theoretical amusement. It aims to illuminate current problems which demand better explanation.

Welcome to SNOWDIDA

For a concrete example of a patriarchal cooking pot, it would be most useful to look at the real-life world of a particular development agency and its programmes in a specific country. Therefore, I shall take the reader to Snowdia, a very isolated nation in the North which no foreigner (except myself) has ever visited. Snowdia has its own government development agency, SNOW-DIDA, which is an administrative extension of the Ministry of Foreign Affairs in the Republic of Snowdia.

We shall look at SNOWDIDA's development activities in the People's Republic of Sundia, one of the least-developed countries in Southern Africa.[2]

Policy evaporation

Imagine a gender consultant who has been called in to look at how gender issues are addressed in a SNOWDIDA programme in Sundia. The consultant is instructed to look at the SNOWDIDA Country Programme. This provides a summary of the overall policy and goals, and of the objectives and activities of all the projects in the SNOWDIDA-supported programme. Table 1 summarises the consultant's assessment of the level of attention to gender issues in the SNOW-DIDA Country Programme in Sundia.

Looking at the 'gender assessment' shown in Table 1, the reader may get the uneasy feeling of already having visited Sundia, or at least somewhere very similar. The assessment shows a gradual diminution as the programme moves from policy statement to policy implementation. This process of diminution is here called *policy evaporation*.

One common aspect of policy evaporation is that, although the policy goals are concerned with women's increased 'participation and control over resources', project objectives have re-interpreted this as 'increased access to resources'. The (bottom–up) strategy of women's participation and empowerment has been reversed into a (top–down) strategy of service-delivery.

Gender-policy evaporation is a common phenomenon. Sometimes the policy evaporates bit by bit, between the formulation of a policy and its implementation. Sometimes you have only to turn over a page of a development plan, and all the gender issues previously mentioned

Table 1: SNOWDIDA Country Programme for Sundia: gender assessment

Aspect of programme	Assessment
Programme Policy	Policy rationale is mainly concerned with supporting government policy and endeavours. There is a brief mention of SNOWDIDA interest in supporting the process of women's empowerment, which is defined as women's increased participation in the development process and increased control over resources.
Situational Analysis	There is some identification of gender gaps, mainly in access to resources and skills training. There is no mention of gender discrimination, or lack of women's representation in decision-making positions.
Programme Goals	Here there are several goals which are concerned with women's increased access to resources, and increased participation in the development process.
Project Goals	There are no specific gender-oriented objectives. When a target group is mentioned, this is sometimes followed by the phrase 'especially women'.
Project Activities	There are no activities which are gender-specific, nor which are concerned with closing gender gaps, overcoming discrimination, or increasing women's participation in the process of project planning and implementation.
Project Implementation	Despite the Country Director's claim that the projects are implemented in a 'gender-sensitive' way, the consultant's visits to various project sites reveal that there is no attempt to identify and address gender issues during the implementation process.

have suddenly disappeared. Evaporation can be a very rapid process!

But this is only the surface evidence of policy evaporation. Now we come to the more interesting question: who is doing what, and why?

Is SNOWDIDA a bureaucracy?

We cannot entirely understand SNOWDIDA's treatment of gender issues if we regard SNOW-DIDA as a normal bureaucracy. This is because bureaucracy is supposed to implement policy. According to the 'proper' theory of bureaucracy, evaporation of policy cannot be understood, since the purpose of the bureaucracy is to implement policy, not evaporate it. More specifically, from a Weberian theoretical perspective of bureaucracy, policy evaporation is incomprehensible at three levels: policy, planning, and organisation. Let us look at each of these in turn.

Policy

SNOWDIDA does not make policy. Policy is made at the political level of government, and the job of SNOWDIDA is to implement policy. According to the Weberian theory of bureaucracy, implementation of policies is the central purpose of the chain of command (from the government). Bureaucratic rules and procedures are primarily concerned with ensuring that policy guidelines from the top generate appropriate action throughout the organisation. It follows that wilful policy evaporation within SNOWDIDA cannot be explained within Weberian theory.

When a SNOWDIDA official dilutes or ignores the policy on women's advancement, the official is actually re-making policy. Negation of a policy automatically becomes policy intervention, entailing the assumption of powers which are not given in the chain of command and which therefore contradict a basic principle of bureaucracy.

Whereas in other areas an official's repudiation of policy would merit dismissal, in the area of women's advancement the official may instead be praised for being honest and pragmatic. There must a different value system operating here. *Something else is going on.*

Planning

Similarly, policy evaporation during the planning process is incomprehensible, according to Weberian principles. The bureaucratic planning process works according to given rules and procedures. Development plans are formulated to address the problems which have been identified in the process of setting the development policy against the facts of the reality in Sundia.

This identification of problems should lead to the formulation of goals, since goals should be concerned with overcoming the problems. Goals give way to objectives which will address the problems. This is part of a logical planning sequence which is an essential aspect of the due process of a Weberian bureaucracy.

Therefore, the gradual evaporation of policy during the planning process is bureaucratically irrational. It entails slippage from the rationality of the proper process, and this slippage contradicts a basic ideal of Weberian bureaucracy. It can be understood only as a mistake, which must be corrected if procedures are being followed properly. However, if there is a *pattern* of evaporation throughout the area of policy on women's advancement, then this cannot be a mistake. *There must be other norms operating, quite outside bureaucratic norms.*

Organisation

A third aspect of Weberian-style bureaucracy is that it adapts to new policy and new demands by developing specialised departments, staffed by professionals with specialised training. But when one asks the SNOWDIDA office in Sundia why the Country Programme has overlooked gender issues, the answer is likely to come back like a shot: 'We have nobody with the training to understand these things'.

The policy has been in place for ten years, and still there are no personnel with the training to implement it? This is incomprehensible within a

Weberian theory of bureaucracy. It demands some other form of explanation. For, from a Weberian perspective, bureaucrats' official opinions are formed only in terms of given policies, and given rules and procedures. Officially, they do not have their own personal opinions; or, if they do, their opinions must not interfere with their work. For Weber, the whole point of a modern bureaucracy is that it made a break with earlier and medieval systems of administration which were patrimonial, patriarchal, autocratic, arbitrary, inconsistent, irrational, and so on. Thus the whole point of a modern bureaucracy is that it follows policy and due process, *and there is not something else really going on.*

Overt bureaucracy and covert patriarchy

It is not enough to say that policy evaporation occurs in SNOWDIDA's programmes because SNOWDIDA is a bureaucracy, and bureaucracies are automatically patriarchal. On the contrary, the bureaucrats are trained to follow rules and procedures, and to implement policies. And yet, if SNOWDIDA adhered to bureaucratic rules, it would actually be implementing the policy on women's advancement. Therefore, SNOWDIDA encompasses two very different forms of organisation: the overt and the covert.

• The overt organisation is the development-agency bureaucracy, with its explicit policies and procedures, and legal-rational system of analysis. The Weberian model is its legitimating ideology.

• The covert patriarchy, or the 'patriarchal pot', is within the organisation, which runs counter to the Weberian model and enables the subversion of those policies and directives which threaten covert patriarchal interests.

When presented with feminist policies, the overt and the covert organisations have opposing interests, values, rules, and objectives: bureaucratic principles demand implementation; patriarchal principles demand evaporation.

The culture of the patriarchal pot

If we apply the label 'patriarchal pot' to the organisation which subverts female gender interests, we need to understand more about the way in which the patriarchal pot can exist alongside the bureaucracy, given that they would seem to be antagonistic. We need to know more about the structure and behaviour of the pot, and how it maintains its existence.

Let us look at the interests which are served by the pot, and the procedures by which it is maintained. If it is actually antagonistic to bureaucracy, we need to know how this contradictory and cancerous state of affairs can continue to survive and thrive in partnership with bureaucracy.

Internal interests of the patriarchal pot

The patriarchal interests within SNOWDIDA are not hard to find. First, of course, like other bureaucracies North and South, it is male-dominated. Gender inequality in recruitment, conditions of service, and promotion are essential for maintaining the SNOWDIDA tradition of male domination and male culture. SNOWDIDA is run as a wing of the Snowdian Ministry of Foreign Affairs, which has always been a male preserve.

Implementing a development policy for women's advancement therefore threatens the male domination of SNOWDIDA. It immediately suggests the need to recruit more women and — even more threatening — to recruit feminists. Herein lies the internal threat to SNOWDIDA: that feminist recruits would not confine their interests to the advancement of women within Sundia, but would be equally interested in the advancement of women within SNOWDIDA!

External interests of the patriarchal pot

Here we have to understand the common patriarchal interest between SNOWDIDA and its cooperating Ministry, the Sundian Ministry of Planning (MOP). Both are government bureaucracies, and, therefore, both have common experience and procedures when it comes to delaying, subverting, or ignoring government policies which threaten the privileges of class, tribe, religious group, gender, and so on. In fact, when it comes to subverting Weberian ideals of legal-rational behaviour, the Sundian Ministry outdoes SNOWDIDA.

In the area of gender, the Sundian MOP has exactly the same problem as SNOWDIDA. It also has a government which, at the political level, has handed down policies on women's equality and advancement. In fact, MOP officials have a more serious interest in ensuring policy evaporation: the government policy on gender threatens not only male domination within MOP, but also the continuance of the patriarchal control of society as a whole. The Sundian government policy on gender equality would challenge the customary laws and traditions which have always maintained male domination of Sundian society.

Whereas the North–South relationship has many underlying conflicts and tensions, common patriarchal interests can provide the basis for brotherhood.

The men's club alliance

The easy and cosy relationship between the officials of SNOWDIDA and MOP needs also to be understood in terms of the 'men's club' culture to which they both belong. Officials on both sides are part of the Sundian male culture of meetings, cocktail parties, and the golf club.

The men's club infects both the office and the social world of the high-level bureaucrat in Sundia. At the office, the privileged male activity of high-level decision-making is supported by the menial female work of office-cleaning, secretarial services, and document-production. Similarly, at the domestic level, the husband's full-time professional occupation is enabled by the wife, who looks after the home, children, schooling, and shopping. Leisure hours at cocktail parties and golf clubs are financed by the unpaid or exploited labour of the lower classes, especially their female members.

In the Sundian men's club, women are not discussed as equals or even as human beings. Women are sexual objects or commodities, to be hunted as sexual prey or acquired for additional wealth and prestige. SNOWDIDA officials who attempt to introduce policies of gender equality into the development discourse not only upset the workplace, they upset the whole patriarchal culture. In particular, they upset the men's club, which is not only the centre of their social life but also their essential meeting place for informal contacts and influence in Sundia.

The structure of the patriarchal pot

We have now looked at the common interests and culture of the alliance which sustains the patriarchal pot. But we still need to look at how this pot actually works. How are we to understand the process by which a particular policy can evaporate, when other policies do not? We have to look at the structure of the pot in terms of its relationship to the overt bureaucracy and its legitimating theory and ideology.

Diplomacy in defence of patriarchy

The Country Director's simple formula for implementing a SNOWDIDA development-support programme in Sundia is, as far as possible, to reduce SNOWDIDA policy in Sundia to the selection of the particular MOP programmes which SNOWDIDA will support. Such a selection process is usually conducted as if there is complete Snowdian–Sundian consensus on development policy.

However, this smooth diplomatic gloss conceals the need for policy-level negotiation in areas where in fact there is lack of consensus. All SNOWDIDA development principles have implications for changes in the structure of Sundian society. Therefore, all development co-operation between Snowdia and Sundia needs to be based on initial negotiations to ensure that the policy priorities of both sides are being pursued. For example, in the area of SNOWDIDA policy on structural adjustment, policy is enforced by conditionality. On structural adjustment, the Country Director's diplomatic gloss disappears, and he (it is likely to be a 'he') talks tough.

But in the area of gender equality, SNOWDIDA behaves more like a diplomatic mission than a development agency. When it comes to SNOWDIDA gender policy, the Country Director suddenly becomes very diplomatic, and states that 'we cannot interfere with the internal affairs of Sundia'.

When the Country Director talks of structural adjustment, he is in charge of a bureaucracy. When he talks of gender issues, he is in charge of the patriarchal pot.

Theory in support of pot preservation

The most important aspect of preserving the patriarchal pot is that it should remain invisible. One important way of enabling the pot quietly and invisibly to evaporate the policy is to adopt a vocabulary in which a discussion of women's empowerment becomes impossible. This may be achieved by adopting a technical vocabulary which is not appropriate for the analysis — or even the recognition — of the political and ideological dimensions of the development process.

In order to maintain the technical level of discourse, the Country Director has advised all SNOWDIDA staff that, as technical advisers, they should avoid all politically loaded words — especially in writing. They should avoid the phrase 'gender inequality' and instead talk more diplomatically about 'gender differences'. Also the word 'equality' should be replaced by 'equity', or some other non-threatening term.

Another essential element in de-politicising the vocabulary is to reduce the discourse on women's advancement to the level of *providing for women's basic needs and increasing their access to resources*. By this means, awkward words such as 'control' or 'discrimination' can be avoided. The word 'oppression' should in no circumstance be entertained. Within this vocabulary, it is possible to discuss women's advancement *within the existing social system*, and not in terms of the need to reform this system.

Addressing gender issues must be treated as a secondary concern which relates only to improved project efficiency. The project has its own primary purpose, concerned with purely technical objectives of increasing the water supply, improving institutional capacity, or whatever. Gender is to be treated as an 'add-on'. Of course, if it can be added, by the same token it can be subtracted.

The implicit ideology of the patriarchal pot

Here we see that the technical vocabulary of development is ideology masquerading as theory. The underlying ideological principle is that systems of male domination in Sundia are not to be the subject of development interventions. Any such intervention is to be labelled as 'interference'. In the area of gender, SNOWDIDA works within the existing patriarchal structure. (Although there is the awkward ideological contradiction that in other areas the policy is structural adjustment!)

This, of course, must remain covert ideology — for the simple reason that the overt principles are the exact opposite of the covert principles. For both SNOWDIDA and Sundia have explicit development policies concerned with promoting gender equality and ending practices of gender discrimination.

This points to the absolute importance of technical rationalisation as a mode and vocabulary of discourse. Within a technical and non-political vocabulary, the ideological contradiction between policy and practice never comes up for discussion. It remains invisible.

Covert procedures of the patriarchal pot

Policy evaporation cannot remain invisible simply on the basis of applying vocabulary control. For instance, there may be vocal members of the women's movement in both Snowdia and Sundia who want to know why there seems to be no action on SNOWDIDA's policies of women's advancement.

So if a gender issue does actually get on to the agenda, how is it to be dealt with? The answer is that it must apparently be dealt with by normal bureaucratic procedure. But this must be done in such a way that the gender issue will slowly evaporate down to nothing.

The procedures of the patriarchal pot are concerned with mocking bureaucratic procedure, making sure that what goes in never comes out. The patriarchal pot implements a strange slow-motion parody of the procedures of Weberian bureaucracy. What looks on the surface like bureaucracy is actually the slow and destructive boiling of the pot.

Let us suppose that a visiting gender consultant has pointed out to the Country Director that family-planning clinics refuse to provide women with contraceptives unless they bring a letter of permission from their husbands. In effect, this makes contraceptives unavailable to most married women and to all single women. And a major part of the SNOWDIDA Health Sector budget is to provide support for family-planning clinics.

The consultant seems to have revealed the lack of attention to the SNOWDIDA gender policy on ending discriminatory practices. The Country Director has to respond to this criticism, and may even have to be seen to take action and make changes in the office. There are various ways in which the Country Director may do this. We may divide his responses into three types of action: verbal defence, diversionary action, and organisational change.[3]

Let us look at each of these in turn. If possible, the Country Director will want to confine his reaction to *verbal defence*, which involves demonstrating that the consultant's criticisms of the programme are mistaken.

Procedures for verbal defence

Denial: The Country Director claims that 'The gender consultant was here for only a day, and has misunderstood the problem. It is Sundian policy that contraceptives are made available only to couples. Therefore, the clinic is only following government policy, to which SNOWDIDA also must also conform.' (But flat denial is a dangerous strategy for the Country Director, because it usually involves

obvious lies. Success depends on the triumph of authority over truth.)

Inversion: 'There is a problem here, but it originates in the home and not in the clinic. It is husbands who insist that wives cannot be given contraceptives without their permission, and Sundian wives accept this situation. This is therefore a domestic problem, in which the Sundian government cannot interfere, let alone SNOWDIDA.' (This should be recognised as yet another version of the old strategy of blaming the victim.)

Policy dilution: 'SNOWDIDA policy is concerned with increasing access to resources, which we have done by providing more clinics and stocking them with a variety of contraceptives. The rules of who is eligible to receive contraceptives must remain in the hands of the government.' (It is not true that SNOWDIDA policy is limited to providing resources to government. The policy also involves enabling women's empowerment and overcoming the obstacles of discriminatory practices.)

Since verbal defence must entail misrepresentation, the Country Director may choose alternative procedures, admitting the problem and proposing action to address it. This is the basis of *diversionary action*.

Procedures for diversionary action

Lip service: 'The consultant has pointed to a problem which has been worrying us for some time. We are most grateful for her clear analysis of the problem. We intend to establish a Consultative Committee to look at these recommendations, which have implications for improving our attention to gender issues in all SNOWDIDA programmes.' (This is often a procedure for sounding good at the time, but with absolutely no intention of taking any action.)

Research study: 'The consultant has pointed to just one aspect of a larger problem, which is very sensitive and touches on matters of Sundian custom and tradition. We have decided to appoint a team from the Sundian Research Institute to look at gender issues in all sectors, in the context of structural adjustment, and to make recommendations on the implications for SNOWDIDA.' (By the time the report comes out, at the end of next year, the original problem should have been forgotten.)

Shelving: 'The research report "Gender Issues in the Context of Structural Adjustment in Sundia" has recently been completed. It has been sent to headquarters in Snowdia for their consideration.' (The report has been shelved. It will never be seen again.)

Procedures for ineffectual organisational change

Even more diversionary is organisational change. This will require significantly more time, which is viewed as a positive aspect on the road to doing nothing. Moreover, if the organisational change is inappropriate for addressing gender issues, there never will be any appropriate outcomes.

Compartmentalisation: 'We are now establishing the new post of Women in Development (WID) Counsellor to head the new WID Section in the SNOWDIDA office in Sundia. The WID Counsellor will advise on gender issues in all projects, will supervise the planning of support for women's projects, and will be in charge of gender training for SNOWDIDA staff and counterparts.' (Since the SNOWDIDA office is divided into conventional sectors, the creation of a separate WID Section effectively treats gender as a separate sector, when it is actually supposed to be an inter-sectoral concern. This compartmentalisation contradicts the SNOWDIDA policy of mainstreaming gender issues in all sectors of development assistance.)

Subversion: 'I have appointed our Programme Assistant, Mrs Patrison, to take on the additional responsibility of WID Counsellor in our office here in Sundia. I know she is very young and has no previous experience in gender issues. But I am sure she will soon pick it up.' (This appointment is an act of pure cynicism. Patrison is a junior official well known for incompetence and administrative confusion, and famous for immediately losing any document given to her.)

Tokenism: 'I am pleased to announce that the wife of the Vice-President, Mrs Charity Wander-Wander, has agreed to sit on our Sundia–SNOWDIDA Health Programme Committee. Until now the Sundian members of this Committee have all been men, but now we shall hear the woman's voice on some of these difficult issues concerning tradition and custom.' (Mrs Wander-Wander is a well-known traditionalist. In fact, she is known for telling women to obey their husbands. Mrs Wander-Wander has been invited as a token woman. In any meeting she will be allowed to speak for five token minutes to ensure that 'the woman's point of view has been heard' before the men take their decision.)

Conclusion

To examine the process of gender-policy evaporation, this paper has introduced the notion of a development agency as a 'patriarchal pot'. A development agency is here seen as a complex cooking pot, on which the lid normally remains closed. The pot is filled with patriarchal bias, implicit in the agency's values, ideology, development theory, organisational systems, and procedures. This is the pot into which policies for women's advancement are thrown. It is a strange patriarchal pot, with much input but no output. Officially the policy exists, and the pot does not. But this paper says that the policy has evaporated, and what remains is the pot.

International programmes for the advancement of women must be based on an analysis of the various forms of patriarchal opposition to gender-oriented policies. In particular, we must take an interest in the workings of government bureaucracies. If we want to change the world, we cannot treat bureaucracy as politically neutral. This paper has analysed the way in which bureaucracy can play a major role in the maintenance and social reproduction of patriarchy. Women's global advancement depends on the transformation of patriarchal bureaucracy into feminocracy, beginning with development agencies.

In other words, as we know more about the patriarchal cooking pot, we must prepare to break it to pieces.

Notes

1 This is a shortened version of a presentation at the seminar 'Women's Rights and Development: Vision and Strategy for the Twenty-first Century', organised by One World Action, Oxfam UK and Ireland, the Gender Institute of the London School of Economics, and Queen Elizabeth House, at the University of Oxford in May 1995. The original paper appears in *Women's Rights and Development*, edited by Mandy Macdonald and published by Oxfam UK and Ireland.

2 Some readers may be familiar with some aspects of Sundia from my discussion of an earlier visit in 'Towards Better North–South Communication on Women's Development: Avoiding the Roadblocks of Patriarchal Resistance', presented at a Women in Development Europe workshop on gender planning, February 1992, Dublin. I am grateful to my partner, Roy Clarke, for the endless discussions which led to the invention of Snowdia and Sundia. My analysis of patriarchal resistance within development agencies was carried further in 'Breaking the patriarchal alliance: governments, bilaterals and NGOs', *Focus on Gender* 2:3 (1995).

3 An earlier interpretation of these 'procedures' appears in Sara Longwe (1990): 'From Welfare to Empowerment: The Situation of Women in Development in Africa', *Women in International Development*, Working Paper No 204, University of Michigan at East Lansing, a paper originally written for the 1988 inaugural meeting of the African Women's Development and Communication Network (FEMNET), Nairobi.

The author

Sara Hlupekile Longwe is a consultant in women's development and an activist for women's rights. She has published widely in the area of gender analysis, and is on the Editorial Board of *Gender and Development*. This article was first published in *Development in Practice* Volume 7, Number 2, in 1997.

Framing participation:
development projects, professionals, and organisations

David Craig and Doug Porter

Holding out the possibility of emancipation, Modern Institutions at the same time create mechanisms of suppression, rather than actualisation, of the self.
(Anthony Giddens, *Modernity and Self-Identity*)

Development projects need to be 'doubly accountable'. They need to be accountable to intended participants and create real opportunities for people to take the project in directions which seem to them most appropriate. But projects must also be accountable to the source of funds which underwrite these opportunities. Projects, in other words, have to be effectively managed.

The two aims, participation and effective management, are deeply contradictory. Participation means fostering local initiative and control; management often requires meeting certain objectives, many already established long before the project begins, maintaining accountability and central control. Generally, projects tend to be more 'managed' than 'participatory', and the balance of control (and project resources and funds) ends up inside the organisations which are managing the projects. Those whom the project is designed to help participate very little, and gain access to a very small proportion of the project's resources.

In recent years, several important organisational bridges have been thrown across this gap, in an attempt to make management more participatory, and participation more formalised in the way in which management occurs. PRA techniques, Process Consultation, decentralisation,

attention to issues of good governance, an increased role for NGOs in development, and attempts to promote civil society as an intermediary between government and the people are all part of attempts to deal with this problem of 'double accountability'. These measures are based on good intentions and a realisation that participation is essential to the success of projects and programmes. They look participatory from a distance, but at close quarters these measures, we believe, actually do little to tip the balance back towards participation. Instead, they have effectively become new forms of management and control, which are just as costly but do not result in great benefits for project participants.

We argue that this situation has arisen because the dominance of three integral, related components has been taken for granted in development: projects, professionals, and organisations. These three components involve certain practices and processes which are primarily instruments of control, rather than of participation. Right from the outset of development projects, professionals and organisations construct a framework of control for potential participants, which rigidly shapes and bounds the kind of participation that is possible, and the directions in which people can go with development projects. It is clear that some local people are better able than others to make themselves and their needs visible within the narrow categories of the frames which these controlling factors produce. But the majority do not, and for this reason we argue that the 'control' aspect of development is perhaps much more pervasive than is widely recognised.

Any attempts to generate more participation will require a fundamental change in the operations of development projects, professionals, and organisations. New forms of project and organisation and new types of professional would be required. Sorting this out is beyond the scope of this article, and our ability. Meantime, we think it is important to pay attention to the ways in which the current tools of participatory development, including PRA, can be used to promote either participation or control, depending on how we use them.

Projects, organisations, and professionals

Development discourse has always given special privilege to its best-performing instruments: projects, organisations, and professionals. These have been seen as so essential for local-level articulation of global development that they are the most commonly invoked conditions placed on 'aiding' development. It was believed that, through these instruments, the task of 'development' could be turned into a series of technical (and thus politically neutral) organisational processes and bounded, manageable objectives. As Apthorpe (1986:379) said of project documents, proposals, sector plans and the like, 'what is involved is apparently ... a completely neutral and purely instrumental form of utterance'.

Within this larger frame, for many observers, *development projects* became development itself, as evident in an oft-quoted definition from Albert Hirschman's book *Development Projects Observed* (1967: 1):

The development project is a special kind of investment. The term connotes purposefulness, some minimum size, a specific location, the introduction of something qualitatively new, and the expectation that a sequence of further development moves will be set in motion ... Development projects ... are the privileged particles of the development process.

As we will see, projects are a particularly powerful way of binding together particular purposes, ideas, resources along with people and places.

Development organisations are diverse, yet distinctive, highly specialised forms of organisation. They became extraordinarily influential during the 1980s, when many heavily indebted nations relied on grants and soft loans to maintain even basic services to their populations. Among development agencies, non-government organisations (NGOs) became prominent, because international and bilateral government donors believed they could reach people and places which government could not, and could thereby help to mediate their concerns for marginal groups of people. Northern NGOs diversified their focus, and replicated their own organisational forms and mechanisms in local counterpart organisations. In the 1990s, global organisations of the United Nations system have moved into deeper and wider engagements, from global military peace-keeping, to the enacting of global charters in diverse social and environmental arenas, to a greater interest in governance and civil society.

Development professionals (or 'technical assistance experts' in 1950s terms) provided a rational and mobile means to direct the capital, technology, and rationality through projects into developing countries. UN Resolutions of the early 1950s endorsed the view that 'defective knowledge and consequent inability to make rational plans' was a major 'constraint'. Technical assistance, through development professionals, was projected as 'democracy's route for expediting' development with 'administrative integrity', which was an important attraction, given the sensitivities of newly independent nations to neo-colonialism. Development professionals have been seen as the 'keys' to successful development, as 'linch-pins of development', 'builders of order', 'catalysts and inducers of economic and social change' (Porter 1995). Here, we consider several kinds of development professional and talk in particular about desk and programme officers and short-term consultants.

The project as frame

Development projects face the difficult task of creating a recognisable, bounded, integrated whole out of some complex ingredients: local geography, community, and economics, project 'inputs' (including people), and the procedures and mechanisms for changing the world that we call development practice. This task has been made all the more difficult because the ends are presented with considerable wholeness and simplicity: incomes must increase, health and welfare have to improve, democracy and good governance have to be fostered, and all in a sustainable way that allows a fair share for women, minorities, the environment, and any other interest that tends to be missed out when Development goes off course. It is hardly surprising that development projects have evolved as a set of strong formal procedures, documents, and techniques. Only these hold out the hope that the project reality might be framed and constructed, and 'development' itself ritually achieved.

Development projects are designed in terms of a number of conventional rationalities. These are *performative*, in that they define ideals, goals, fields, and mechanisms of project activities. These rationalities generally are of two different but mutually dependent kinds. The first are *project goals*, which reflect implicit values such as empowerment or growth, or improvement in the satisfaction of 'needs'. Unlike, but implicit in, the specific objectives and inputs of projects, these ideals are timeless and highly moral. 'Improved standards of living and peace and order' reads the goal statement of one project, typical of many. The second kind of rationality is the *specific objectives* of the project. These are generally observable, objectively defined ends which are to be realised by the specific mechanisms of the project. They include target populations and areas (beneficiaries), and are logically linked to the supply of resources or inputs, a limited number of desired outputs, and a list of specific project activities carried out over the duration of the project.

Together, the goals provide the rationale for the objectives and mechanisms or activities. They make all project activities and objectives appear legitimate, because of their links with the high ideals of development. In turn, objectives are intended to reconstruct the local community in the image of the overall goal, which typically is closely affiliated with higher ideals. This combination of objectivities and ideals provides a compelling, flexible framework, that is at once idealistic *and* practical, but is also unlimited *and* specific. The two, objectives and ideals, are mutually reinforcing, and the presence of both enables embattled project officers to move back and forth between each, as needs for justifications and performance arise.

The key point is that, while all projects require this combination of ideals and concrete objectives, the ability of local people to express their own desires and needs in these terms is often limited. The project, however, selects and presents what local people say in terms of these requirements. Desires and interests that do not fit are simply not recorded. People who are best at expressing themselves within the high moral and technical frame of the project will thus have greater influence. This is why educated élites, and males, tend to expect and get a greater portion of the project's resources to flow in their direction.

Further framing of local people and their concerns and interests is also carried on within the project. Within the project frame, the population of development beneficiaries and participants is represented within social, economic, and demographic categories, each of which stabilises and homogenises specific people within larger groups. These homogenising, taxonomic categories include locality, 'the community', the household, and particular groups such as women; or, within them, 'sub-categories', such as Commercial Sex Workers, or petty traders. These categories are designed to include all relevant subjects in a particular group, and this further reinforces the project's claims to political representativeness and a broad-based legitimacy.

Again, these categories come from outside, along with the project. They make it clear that if any individuals are to participate in the project, they must present themselves within the framework of terms required by it. Clearly, some groups are less visible within this frame than others. Marginal groups are easily left unrecognised, even where the project is focused on women or the poor. Important family connections which overlap categories may not be visible within the frame. Thus close relatives of an élite person may be able to get access to project resources designated for the poor, because they are in a position to adapt themselves to fit the project's categories.

The population is assumed to be reasonably stable in geographical terms for the duration of the project. Indeed, many projects have been formulated with the express aim of keeping itinerant populations in a particular place; for instance, social and agricultural services are frequently provided to reduce migration or to hold itinerant populations in designated resettlement areas. This stabilising effect is generally welcome to anyone with the responsibility of administering or governing populations or territories. Marginal people, however, often lack a stable local base, and can easily fall through or move (or be moved) out of the categories provided by the project frame.

The project frame also locates people in relation to certain explicitly valued *practices* which are made specific in the project, and with which compliance is gauged as a measure of the project's success or otherwise. First are standardised measures and assessments of local practices, which are becoming more common with the advent of international standards and benchmarking (ISO 9000, total quality management). For instance, agricultural development projects typically feature 'farming systems analysis', baseline surveys, 'PRAs', or 'training needs assessments' as part of the mandatory ensemble of practices necessary for 'getting the facts straight' and for calibrating the inputs to the local situation. Similarly, HIV/AIDS intervention projects most often apply KAPB (Knowledge, Attitudes, Practices, Behaviours) surveys as the means whereby the categories (such as Commercial Sex Workers) are 'filled in' with specific values and behaviours, frequently based on assumptions about these in Western societies (Plummer and Porter 1997).

The population, inputs, and outputs are located within a *time frame*, the project cycle. This cycle is segmented and sequenced, with specific activities, practices, budgetary inputs, observations (project reviews and evaluations), outputs, and re-conceptualisations scheduled into it. Feasibility study comes before design, and after this comes implementation, and so on. Again, certain people are more easily able to organise themselves at

particular times to get their interests included; to fit themselves to the project's time frame. Others may not, at crucial times in the project cycle, be able to be there and so participate.

The attempt to replicate development values, objectives, and practices, often in very different local situations, constitutes a form of control — or, put differently, a form of 'governance at a distance' (Rose and Miller 1992). This replication has become, in many circles, the 'essence' of what good development practice is about. Projects are typically evaluated in terms of how well they initially framed the local situation and brought about stable outcomes in accordance with the early frame of the project.

The professional as framer

In practical terms, the space between donor and recipient is traversed by organisations through global communications media, and (our focus here) by the employment of particular varieties of development professional: desk or programme officers, and short-term consultants. These professionals provide development organisations with mobile, authoritative means of overseeing the transfer of goals, objectives, information, resources, and practices that need to travel and be locally replicated for the project to be realised. Their particular roles, their professional kudos, and the practices they have formed for dealing with the chaos that regularly confronts them constitute another significant framing mechanism for the development enterprise.

The raw material with which these development practitioners work in developing project proposals has usually already been pre-selected as generally fitting within the frame of the interests and perceived capabilities of their organisation, and also within larger frames of donor-selected sectors or initiatives, such as women and development (WID) or country priorities. Within this, however, desk and programme officers generally work in an atmosphere of uncertainty and scrappy knowledge. Typically based in donor countries, or in metropolitan centres of developing countries, professionals employed by development agencies rely on variously constructed proposal documents, observations from local counterparts, and (often brief) 'field visits' for their information.

Documentation usually involves scrambling to fill in the standard format categories from the donor's protocols, fitting the often fluid, fragmentary details of the local situation to the overarching, framing story of need, opportunity, and willingness, as well as to the technical language of standardised project-proposal forms. Local quirks of situation or language must be turned into something accounted for and recognised, even when the extent of possible difficulties is not yet known.

In framing documents, close adherence to the framework of donor guidelines offers some security: filling in all the categories asked for, framing the project in terms of donors' current interests, relying on past experience (perhaps on an unrelated project in another part of the world), and on other conventional knowledge of what is acceptable.

A range of ritual, documentary techniques is now available to create the impression of order, and to provide confidence as the project moves from pre-feasibility studies to project design, implementation, and evaluation phases. Initially, conventional development objectives must be abstracted from the morass of local culture and community. Because these will be the basis of subsequent scrutiny of the project by others, they need to be framed as solidly as possible, providing the indicators of time (by when things will be achieved), space (where, geographically and institutionally), responsibility (by whom and with what chains of accountability upwards to the funding agency), and quantities of inputs, mentioned above, all well ahead of schedule, and often with little resort to a close knowledge of field conditions.

Rendering the document in a Logframe (or Logical Framework), or producing projected cost-benefit analyses performs a parallel back-up or safety-check role. By providing an apparently technically sophisticated analysis and planning format, the ritual suggests to project appraisers that uncertainties have been submitted to the frame of an authoritative planning technology. The Logframe format also gives programme officers the chance to gesture at and name external influences in a way that allows in advance for points of excuse or exit, when local

realities during implementation throw things off course and erode the certainty of the original project statement. Biographical data of key project personnel are appended to proposal documents, conveying the same ritualistic, fabulous impression of authority and experience for the project that they do for the people themselves.

Desk or programme officers' personal and organisational career fortunes are mixed in with the fortunes of the project; promotion in some organisations comes through getting numbers of projects funded, and the threat of a job in, say, the archives department or the contracts section hangs over the head of the officer with the notoriously bad project. Their dependence on local managers, national counterparts, and local organisations creates tension, and an incentive to see that local agents and resources are tied down as much as possible, to fit the frame.

Programme officers are thus deployed by their organisations to order and represent local situations in terms of the organisation's own rationalities and priorities. By standing out from the locals when they visit (with their logo T-shirts, laptop computers, or white skin), they also provide an organisational — even a national — presence and identity for the project, as required by organisational publicists and official donors alike.

In practice, the professionals' work is more than a translation: it is a production, large parts of which must be achieved without the subjects of development. They must construct an entire theatrical scenario for the project, including the dramatic conceit, the sequences of plot, the set and props, and the casts of stars, and of thousands of 'extras'.

Framing, political legitimacy, and governance at a distance

The use of local partner organisations is perhaps the most salient feature of development involving NGOs in recent years; they are variously termed Rural-Based Organisations, Member-Accountable Organisations, People's Organisations, and so on. The 'main game' in development — in terms of funding, projects, and people — obviously still occurs well away from here, outside the NGO world; but NGOs' increasing prominence is indicative of the organisational refinement of governance through development during the second half of the 1980s.

Typically, an NGO-related development project will involve a funding body, a metropolitan intermediary, a partner intermediary NGO in the developing country, and at least one level of local organisation. Each of these re-frames and reconstitutes the project in terms of its own concerns and priorities, and practical capacity. The project, as framed and agreed on by funding and metropolitan intermediary organisations, is subject to a number of reformulations before its objectives can become visible in and to the target population.

Project objectives and goals are supposed to travel down the length of this chain of organisations, and be reproduced intact within the target population. However, at each point on this chain, the project is filtered and re-framed to fit the objectives and categories of the organisation at that level. Local difference thus gets reduced to simple categories and objectives, often, so it appears, more for the primary benefit of the framing organisation than for the purposes of supporting local initiative and participation.

At one end of the chain is the funding organisation, which has strongly developed mechanisms for the filtering and re-interpretation of local and other project proposals. Each of these is linked to the availability of funds, and thus crucially to the project's possibilities. Funding, for example, is available for some 'sectors' and not others; this year, one 'initiative' is named; next year, another. Environmental initiatives followed appropriate technology; 'women in development' came next; then a more embracing concern with sustainable human development. Each sector and initiative typically includes particular objectives which define it as being *this* sector or initiative, and not some other. However, different agendas, with uneven filtering and opportunistic translation of local situations and rationalities at each organisational point along the chain, ensure that this transition is not as smooth and simple as represented here.

Development organisations must be able to represent themselves to funders and beneficiaries alike as the embodiment and means of the realisation of development ideals such as justice and care. They typically represent their field of operations as encompassing the poor and needy, perhaps of a particular region. They claim a legitimacy by being able to be seen to transform the lives of needy people, to access and alter the physical, social, and economic aspects of their lives in a sustainable, democratic way. This representation and the political positioning it entails are crucial: funders must be able to see that their requirements are mirrored in their counterpart organisations, all the way down the chain.

The local organisation and its members provide the NGO intermediary with a locally legitimate presence, as well as a base from which to move universal development practices into the locality and population. Each level of organisation reproduces the framing logics of the organisation above it, but at a cost. Partner organisations in-country, however, can claim to be local, so that their organisational costs, which often take a large share of project funds, can be shown as in-country costs by the donor NGO. Partnership with a local or in-country NGO also shifts responsibility from the intermediary NGO on to some local figures, and provides an alibi for its eventual disengagement, either at the end of the project cycle or before, if the relationship between organisations or with locals turns sour. Bad projects can be put down to institutional capacity-building for counterparts.

NGOs must negotiate with local subjects in order to incorporate them on the terms of the objectives they are given. They must aim to secure local agreement, and/or at least visible compliance with desired rationalities and practices. This negotiation links, with various effects, officially and politically sanctioned goals, objectives, and practices with local people and places that hitherto were not within their reach. NGOs have the ability to make disparate constituencies accessible; they speak the language at both ends, and can represent one in terms of the other. While representation and mediation can benefit local communities, other outcomes are always a real possibility.

In order to achieve their widely cast goals, then, organisations must get down to practice. Unlike vision, practice is resource-dependent and involves specific, limited people, trying to make the best of a situation that is not as simple as the project documents claim. This tying together is by no means always entirely successful. There are agency costs (time, frustration) associated with supervision and motivation, and not all employees are able to realise the organisation's practical objectives. Local people's participation may be crowded out by executive expertises and control of practices and finances. Or they may simply not have time or incentive to participate as hoped.

Fortunately for the organisation, however, the events supposedly set in train by projects are seldom evaluated for long-term sustainability. What is sustained is the organisation, and its organising, framing practices.

Nevertheless, the work of public representation must go on, as it generates the organisation's income. Loose ends are tidied away, and failures represented and filed (internally to the organisation) as lessons learned. Successes are trumpeted to supporters and funders in reports and promotional material, but very little is done to ensure that a close analysis of the mechanisms that led to the success is made available to other organisations. Attempts at 'replication' may follow: the reproduction of the same organisation's project in a geographically and socially different (though close enough) locale. A good KAPB (that is, a published one) on an HIV/AIDS intervention project in Vietnam is quickly used to legitimate the same in another project in Burma (Myanmar). Occasionally, one organisation's success becomes a benchmark and model for others to follow. At present, however, a good deal more might be done to ensure the flow of useful information over the boundaries formed by organisational frames.

Conclusions

Must it be like this? Must the multiple framing mechanisms always carry the day, circumscribing creative agency, and bounding participation?

As it happens, of course, in the less than ideal world of everyday project reality, the local participants rarely engage with our ideals and objectives in quite the way we intended. They do not fully disengage from their own dreams and ideals, but bring them along on the project journey, and try to realise them within the confined space of the project. In terms of the space, time, and categories

allocated to them by the project, they become 'deviant'; or, by various means of foot-dragging and flight, they resist. As development workers, we are poorly equipped to deal with this reality in a positive way, one that can grasp the significance of the richly diverse means by which local people try to capitalise on the opportunities the project might provide. A common response to the deviance is to remind local people of the objectives or, as one Australian development worker confided, to 'nail the bastards to the implementation schedule'. We screw down the resources, so that they don't travel off the course mapped out for them.

Pressures of work mean there is little time, or reward, to think about how the system might be changed, let alone what it would look like if change occurred. Better to find out how to make it work as efficiently as possible, where the shortcuts and loopholes are, and leave it to someone else to make the rules, or the critical comment that might affect the funding. But there is another side to practice.

The creativity with which development professionals approach the framing of projects in order to get them funded suggests that people are not only well aware of the framing process, but are able to manipulate it too. Our experience is that there is much room to move. But to see beyond the framing process, it is necessary to be more deliberately involved in two things: the *creation of space* and *enablement*. The first involves the ethical and political act of creating space to allow the subjects of development to make their own representations and projections, if needs be in opposition to the frames we construct for them. It probably also involves a great deal more rule-bending and subterfuge on the part of development professionals, given that much of the industry is geared to reduce, not expand, the autonomy of local people. Enablement involves a determination to facilitate other people's access to the framing tools of our development; the language, the institutional acumen, the planning technologies. Neither of these two requirements is without instance, but examples in practice seem to have occurred at the behest of the project, where people have seized upon spaces where things are not well defined, or where things can happen when someone else is not looking.

It seems to us that enhancing the space-creating and enabling aspect of practice requires *new skills*, skills that fall well outside the project-planning and management-training courses that tend these days to scoop up the more creative NGO and local-agency development workers in response to the relentless demands for 'professionalism' and 'accountability' to the master framers. And *new organisational forms:* the fostering of local networks on a semi-permanent basis, of encounters between planners and locals who may or may not form an intermediary organisation in their own right.

And finally, activities and skills in development practice which could foster the creation of space and enablement would require *a different outlook*. This has been advocated many times before, and Robert Chambers' 'new professionalism' seems to capture much of what is required (Chambers 1994). But, more than this:

What we desperately need today is to learn to think and act more like the fox than the hedgehog — to seize upon those experiences and struggles in which there are still glimmerings of solidarity and promise of dialogic communities in which there can be genuine mutual participation and where reciprocal wooing and persuasion can prevail. For what is characteristic of our contemporary situation is not just the playing out of powerful forces that are always beyond control, or the spread of disciplinary techniques that are always beyond our grasp, but a paradoxical situation where power creates counter-power and reveals the vulnerability of power, where the very forces that undermine and inhibit communal life also create new, and frequently unpredictable, forms of solidarity. (Bernstein 1983)

References

Apthorpe, R. (1986) 'Development policy discourse', *Public Administration and Development*, 6: 377–89.

Bernstein, R. J. (1983) *Beyond Objectivism and Relativism: Science, Hermeneutics and Praxis*, Oxford: Blackwell.

Chambers, R. (1994) 'Poverty and Livelihoods: Whose Reality Counts', paper to UNDP Stockholm Roundtable, 'Change: Social Conflict or Harmony?', Overview Paper II, mimeo.

Giddens, A. (1991) *Modernity and Self Identity: Self and Society in the Late Modern Age*, Polity.

Hirschman, A. (1967) *Development Projects Observed*, Washington DC: Brookings Institute.

Plummer, D. and D. Porter (1997) 'Epidemiological categories: foundations or fallacies', in G. Linge and D. Porter (eds), *No Place for Borders: HIV/AIDS and Development in Asia and the Pacific*, Sydney: Allen and Unwin.

Porter, D. (1995) 'Scenes from childhood: the homesickness of development discourses', in J. Crush (ed.) *The Power of Development*, London: Routledge.

Rose, N. and P. Miller (1992) 'Political power beyond the State: problematics of government', *British Journal of Sociology*, 43(2): 173–205.

The authors

David Craig is at the National Centre for Development Studies, Australian National University, where he is researching the impact of economic liberalisation on local health and pharmaceutical use in Vietnam.

Doug Porter is Regional Technical Adviser for the UN Capital Development Fund, based in Kampala. He is a Fellow of the National Centre for Development Studies at the Australian National University, and has had a long association with Community Aid Abroad in Indochina, the Philippines, and east Africa.

This article first appeared in *Development in Practice* Volume 7, Number 3, in 1997.

Sustainable development at the sharp end: field-worker agency in a participatory project

Cecile Jackson

The direction of much modern social theory suggests that in development studies we may have been rather too structuralist in our approaches to development policy, programmes, and projects: too concerned with the formal, the planned, the intended, too willing to see institutions as sets of rules and procedures (Giddens 1984; Clay and Schaffer 1984; Long and Long 1992; Booth 1994). Current interest in agency-oriented and actor-oriented analysis of social change suggests, on the other hand, a different vision: of a mutual determination between individual action and social structures, of choice, resistance and struggle, of the power of the apparently weak, of the multiplicity and contingency of perceptions of reality, of the negotiated character of development outcomes rather than the imposition of policy. The implications for development practice include the questioning of the degree to which development plans and policy can ever be 'implemented' in a straightforward way, or the degree to which outcomes relate to intentions; a lesser emphasis on designs, plans, blueprints, and rules and a greater emphasis on enlisting support, often via participation, for shared development aims, on changing attitudes and work cultures so that agency becomes an opportunity rather than a (subversive) constraint. There is a special interest here in the particular experience of the 'street level bureaucrat' (Lipsky 1980), i.e. the person who is at the direct interface of project with people, and the ways in which this shapes their agency, their choices, their interpretations and

strategies, and thereby actively shapes the project. There has been a widespread recognition of the importance of the work cultures, conditions, and relationships of this person, often on the lowest rung of the organisation in terms of status and authority but capable of making, or breaking, a project (Wade 1992, Goetz 1996). Curiously, however, participatory thinking often casts the field-worker as desirably passive, responding to the initiatives of villagers but not imposing his or her own subjectivity. This notion of the field-worker is unrealistic (for no person can efface his or her identity in such a way), and is a potentially costly illusion.

The project context

This paper is a reflection on some social-development issues which have arisen in the first five years of the Rain-fed Farming Project (RFP), Eastern India, funded by ODA.[1] The RFP started in 1989 in three States (Orissa, Bihar, and West Bengal) and was conceived as a project which would 'develop a new approach for the development of rain-fed areas, specifically incorporating the principles of poverty focus, participation, minimum subsidy and the involvement of women' (ODG 1995). The analysis of the failure of the Green Revolution to benefit rain-fed areas mainly emphasised the inability of poor farmers to adopt crop technologies requiring a high input of cash, except where adoption has been induced by heavy subsidies (by which was meant resources offered to farmers at below cost). Genuine participation, and sustainability, were seen in terms of farmer adoption without subsidies. The project aimed to focus on the needs of resource-poor farmers, on development without recourse to subsidies, with the full involvement of women in all aspects of the development process. Participation was conceived as villagers playing 'a full part in the choice, testing, and development of innovations ... [as] the surest way of arriving at low-cost technologies appropriate to villagers' own circumstances' (ODG, 1995:1).

The structure of the project was based on a team consisting of a Cluster Agronomist (CA) and a Village Motivator (VM) covering each cluster of two or three villages, located in the poorest parts of eight poor districts. Each district was coordinated by a District Agronomist (DA), and each of the three States had a Senior Motivator (SM). A Women in Development (WID) cell was established at the Bihar headquarters in Ranchi, and at the head office in Calcutta there were subject specialists (crops, soils, agroforestry), as well as a participation specialist (over a short period), staff engaged in monitoring and evaluation (M&E), and the Project Manager. The CAs were older than the VMs, and had technical skills or qualifications.

The analysis here is based on interviews with field-staff of RFP, carried out on two visits to the project, and on the detailed daily records kept in three field-worker diaries over a period of three to five years. The diaries were kept by all VMs and are official, in that staff were asked by project management to keep them. Thus they are not explicitly personal, and what was written in them no doubt reflected the expectation (at least at the beginning of their employment) that they would be read by their superiors. In practice they were almost never read, however: only two comments (both by consultants, not project managers) were found in one of the three diaries, to indicate that anyone had read it. The diary became a useful record for the VM of activities and discussions and, at times, an outlet for frustrations and concerns which give insights into the field-workers' experience and the operation of the project. VMs were in a structurally weak position within the project and yet, I shall argue, their position at the interface gave them considerable influence in shaping what the project was to become.

The diaries used in this paper refer to three clusters, two in Bihar and one in West Bengal. They are referred to as cluster A and B (both in Hazaribagh District of Bihar) and C (in Purulia District of West Bengal); information from diaries is referenced by location and date.[2] The diaries contain a wide range of material: accounts of on-going project activities; the thoughts and experiences of the VMs; notes on meetings and conversations with villagers; brief reports on items of research. They were kept daily (or nearly) and reveal a 'blow by blow' account of the making of a project. The material has had to be used selectively; here I have selected that which illuminates the subject position of VMs. All three of these diaries were kept by men. I have elsewhere (Jackson 1997) examined the gender-related aspects of the experiences of VMs and participators at this project interface.

Sustainability was conceived as necessary in environmental, social, and political terms. Doing sustainable poverty-reduction through the RFP involved no or minimal subsidies, since low-external-input agriculture was seen as both environmentally sustainable and socially sustainable, since a subsidy-dependent activity cannot endure in poor areas in the absence of State or project intervention. This approach had a number of implications for field-staff. One is that the project tends to be self-targeting towards the poor, since better-off farmers can gain little from direct participation; for example seed quantities distributed are less than a kilogram. Another benefit is that the absence of subsidy allows RFP to remain free from the unwanted attentions of the *panchayats* (elected councils covering groups of five villages), in States where political rivalry at local level results in attempts to monopolise projects for the benefit of particular groups. The absence of subsidised inputs, however, also makes the work of the VM and CA more difficult, for all other development organisations do offer at least payment for labour.

Institutional sustainability was, at the project-design stage, seen as best approached through working with a State-funded institution, such as the Hindustani Fertiliser Corporation (HFC), with permanent staff seconded to work on the RFP. However, such organisations were in the process of being overtaken by history — in the form of economic liberalisation — and HFC has now been replaced by KRIBHCO, a marketing cooperative with western Indian roots, as the management organisation; in this organisation almost all staff are on short-term contracts.[3]

The position of the VM at the interface of the project with village society means that s/he is the person who brokers the deals whereby project and participants cooperate in activities; who interprets the project to the people and *vice versa*; who negotiates differences of opinion; who enlists people into project activities and allows the project to be enlisted into their agendas; who manages the interlocking of the perceived interests of the project and the people. The VM is therefore vital to the project and also carries a peculiar burden of interpretation, being part of two worlds.

The next section describes the shape of the VMs' experience over the first few years of the project, how they enlisted participants and implemented the poverty focus, and the contradictions faced at the sharp end.

Field-worker identity

One insight gained from studying the VM diaries is the realisation of how, over time, a project is shaped through the accumulation of daily interactions of staff and participants. All the diaries record the initial encounters with the poor tribal and low-caste communities in which the VMs went to live, and the problems of communicating what the project was, and who they were, across the divides of language, culture, education, and class. All mention the hostility, fear, and confusion between themselves and the villagers. The VM in cluster A mentions one very common problem when explaining the trial programme: 'Most of the farmers are afraid ... they were saying that their land may be taken away' (A, 9 June 1989). Fear and suspicion are vividly recorded by the VM in cluster B, who wrote in December 1991, when he first went to live there: 'In Borogora farmers simply refused to speak to me.' People ask about his real work and do not believe his account of the RFP; he sadly notes: 'I felt it

bad' (H, 30 December 1991). The people in Borogora were still refusing to talk to him by the end of January 1992, and he records that he went and helped them harvest mustard for a whole day, at the end of which he writes with relief: 'Mr Makadeo Munda smiled.' A few days later they speak to him a little about their declining maize yields, but on his next visit they confront him with a rejection, saying 'We don't want anyone to come into our village.' One older person says: 'We are illiterate and can't read anything so I shall not be able to know what you are writing.' In despair the VM writes: 'I was standing where I had started!' He offered to write nothing. At the end of February the VM records the following exchanges:

Today I went to Badka Karam and they asked me a series of questions. They asked me 'Are you from missionaries?' I said no. I am from HFC who make fertilisers. They looked happy and said 'Well give me a packet of fertiliser'. Then again I told that I am not giving you any fertilisers simply I want to improve your cultivation by good seeds. Then one young man told 'Oh you are VLW![4] I said no. He looked a bit confused.

VMs encountered considerable resistance and fear, and faced real problems in explaining their identity. They needed to establish a new kind of relationship with villagers which had few parallels; it was not based on authority or on hand-outs: it demanded cooperation and trust of a stranger, from people who had little reason to believe the promises of educated and privileged 'outsiders'. The comments recorded in the diaries, and the time and effort taken to open up communication, raise a large question mark over any expectations that poor village people willingly divulge truthful and accurate information in one-off 'participatory' research exercises, and suggests that project initiation is a lengthy process. The VM of cluster B writes of the problems of identity and communication as follows:

In these 8 months I find that to make one's identity like government official is very easy. Like whenever I went to any village they gave me a cot to sit on and offered water to drink. But as far as project philosophy is concerned one has to make rapport ... (and) they should start coming with their own ideas. To charge them to speak something of their own is time taking. (B, 27 February 1992)

He recognises too, with the word 'charge' that he *requires* them to communicate and participate. Clearly village people tried to fit the VM into the role of one of the familiar cast of characters, known if not loved, in rural India. The cast may vary from State to State: in West Bengal, where the peasant vote is courted by politicians, the VM was suspected for a long time of being a politician (some saw his beard as conclusive evidence), a suspicion far from the minds of Biharis, whose democratic clout is largely irrelevant to local politics. These records of first encounters suggest that, even with well-trained and committed staff, a minimal interaction and degree of trust are difficult and slow to establish. The formative experiences of VMs left them desperate to get something going, in a weak bargaining position, and disinclined to make much of the poverty focus.

Mutual enrolment by field-workers and participants

The VM diaries also show the early staking out of positions by actors. The explanations by the VM of the project objectives and the perception by villagers of the dependence of the VM on their cooperation are glimpsed in other comments, such as when a VM records the persistent, explicit, and almost threatening demands for water from villagers: 'Farmers said "If you want to develop, give me well, otherwise nothing can be done"' (B, December 1991). The tenacity of farmers' demands for irrigation is remarkable in all areas: in cluster A, after three years of project involvement, a note in the diary for 3 October 1992 shows that farmers are still asking for pumps and check dams.

The process of mutual enrolment, by persuasion and by threat, eventually involves some kind of compromise in areas of shared interest, but it takes some time to get there. Most VMs faced a double challenge: the misconception that they had more resources on offer than they in fact could command, and the mismatch between what they actually had to offer, given the project

objectives, and what emerged from open discussions with villagers. In discussions of needs, most villagers expressed their wish for irrigation facilities (for example, A, 16 December 1989 and C, 28 April 1992), yet the RFP was committed to crop technologies for dryland development. The RFP agreed with villagers that rain-fed areas were poor because they lacked irrigation, but differed in that the RFP seemed to view irrigation as costly, inequitable, and physically unfeasible for the majority of farmers. The persistent expressions of desire for irrigation reflect the social status of many of those who initially approached, or communicated with, the VM. The VM resistance to enrolment in demands for irrigation was necessary, given the project's focus on poverty, but not comfortable, given the feeling that the project should respond to expressed needs. The apparent contradictions between elements of the project approach have to be resolved by the VM. How does a VM decline enrolment in a villagers' project? One example is recorded for cluster A, where a check dam was being demanded: the VM explained to people that 'The paths will be shown to them and they will have to walk on that path by themselves' (A, 5 May 1989). *How* to decline, though, is probably less difficult than the decisions over *what* to decline.

Project enrolment involved a number of different kinds of participant relations. There were (at least) the relations with ordinary project participants, and those with people who became brokers and facilitators, with a closer involvement and a sense of shared responsibility. Such 'super-participants' seemed to be people who became personal friends of the VM, or especially cooperative individuals who placed a high value on their connection with the project. It would be too crude to suggest that such people were only the powerful, conspiring to turn the project to their own ends; there were also those who had enhanced their social standing through project identification, or for whom the visits of consultants (for there is no doubt that visitors tend to see the same people when they visit) validated their own idea of themselves, or who simply liked and got on well, at a personal level, with the VM. Friends of field-workers tend not to be from the opposite sex, or to cross other major social divides.

Over time, the project and the people, or a selection of them, increasingly accommodate themselves to what is known of the other, and each becomes skilled in representing their wishes in ways which are likely to be more acceptable. For example, in cluster C, farmers learned the discourse of participation and, after four years of the project's existence, presented a suggestion for the purchase of crop-spraying equipment as something 'which will help in group action ... a sprayer can play a vital role in establishing harmony' (C, 28 November 1993). The 'harmony and group action' card was played by these farmers in an attempt to mitigate the agrochemical-input and subsidy-dependent aspects of their request, which are not favoured by the project.

The growing conflation of the personal and professional lives of the village-resident VMs over time is an important feature of field-workers' experience and behaviour. Living in the village removes the usual separation between personal and professional life to a large extent and has considerable implications, which the diaries reveal. The VM in cluster A learns about corruption (A, 9 May 1989) in the withholding of women's wages by contractors, but is unable to do anything about it; on other occasions he notes social problems beyond his control. VMs struggle to defend the boundaries of the personal, and to cope with the discomforts of life and the small but cumulative physical and mental privations of village life. In cluster B, the VM explains that he is so much in view that he cannot eat chicken because it would be tactless, given the poverty of the villagers and his wish to identify with them. This becomes acute in drought years, and he records after a bad year that 'Farmers have nothing to eat, whenever I go to them they ask for food, so they can feed their children' (B, October 1992). On other occasions he has a hard time politely refusing offers of alcoholic drink from tribals (27 January 1992). After the 1993 drought, the VM writes that farmers are coming daily for financial aid and that he 'does not loan but where he can he donates' (19 April 1993). This is clearly a stressful situation, shared by most VMs. As the monsoon fails in cluster C, the VM writes poignantly that 'Everybody is looking to the sky with blank eyes' (C, 2 July 1991). Some VMs do lend money to villagers in need, and at least one took land in return for a loan, which he began to farm.

Field-worker discretion

Field-worker discretion (Goetz 1996) allows the shape of the project to be influenced, to varying degrees, by the personal choices, opinions, and behaviour of staff at the lowest level. Field-worker discretion may be a question of selecting what initiatives the field-worker responds to. The discretionary element, the field-worker agency, is often invisible (Wade 1992), for various reasons: the representation of discretionary choices as determined by project policy, concealment of various kinds, and the tendency for villagers to collude in field-worker representations to outsiders. Added to this is the dominant view in participatory thinking of the field-worker as relatively passive in relation to the active participant. The tip of the discretionary iceberg is seen in some of the field-worker activities which were unsuccessful, in that they attracted a degree of disapproval from other project staff. One direct example is the action taken by a CA in West Bengal who planted *Shabita* (a new paddy variety) at the village tank, i.e. on intensively managed lowland, despite the project emphasis on rain-fed upland crops. He was rebuked by HFC and no further lowland promotion took place; nevertheless, the variety took off as a successful lowland crop.

More indirectly, we get glimpses of field-worker discretion which does not overtly transgress project policy. In Orissa a District Agronomist (DA), using his discretion, tried unsuccessfully to get a canalisation scheme funded by the Block Development Officer (BDO) for a small group of farmers, including the *sarpanch* (the head of the *panchayat*) of one village. Both the DA and the CA complained widely that the BDO had finally failed to approve the scheme, claiming a corrupt reallocation to another applicant. The CA and DA took a series of visiting consultants to see the individual who was to have been the main beneficiary of the scheme, and thereby publicised what they saw as a good initiative which the project (given the approach to subsidies) was unable to support directly. They made it clear that the project approach to such cases, to assist in accessing State BDO funds, failed as a result of the inefficiencies and corruption of the State. Field-worker resistance to the project's approach to subsidies was greater from the agronomists, who were trained within different development paradigms, and who were less concerned about the poverty focus than VMs were. The persistent steerage of visitors to the farmer who did not get the canalisation appeared to be part of a lobbying campaign to bring the issue to the attention of those who might help to redirect the anti-subsidy policy through conceding the value of the canalisation project, the worthiness of the beneficiaries, and the absence of alternatives indicated by the failure of the application for BDO funding. Field-worker discretion can amount to subversion. The use of particular participants as regular contributors and interviewees in consultancy visits is one means by which field-workers can selectively represent their work and lobby for changes in policy.

VM discretion is called into play particularly in the tension between the poverty focus of the project and the social pressures within villages towards interaction with the more prosperous. This took a number of forms: the problem of whether to accept the hospitality of the *Mukiya* — the village head; the unwillingness of poor farmers to stick to agreed locations of trial plots, or to share the seed of successful varieties; the ethical dilemmas of the risk of crop failure in experimentation with poor farmers; the pressures from wealthier farmers for seed, and their sneers at 'crop neglect' by poor farmers. The diaries show VMs' inclinations towards a less rigid focus on poverty and their rehearsal of arguments that 'the project should also include such surplus members who are morally well enough to help the deficit group' (A, 26 June 1991). Discretion in this direction was also exercised in the enthusiasm for 'block planting groups' which involved all contiguous farmers (of whatever status) planting together, and in the manipulation of wealth-ranking, which was carried out so loosely as to classify the vast majority (some 80 per cent) of many villages as deficit, i.e. as the target group.

Overall, the diaries show that the VMs substantially influenced the course of events in the specific project experiences in the three States, but in a complex way, both defending and conceding the poverty focus, depending on circumstances.

Field-worker authority and PRA

One area which demonstrates the limitations on project plans deriving from the particular social position of the VM was the experience with Participatory Rural Appraisal. PRA exercises were conducted by VMs as the basis for workplans; but, despite the PRA training, widely held to be well done with plenty of practical work, and visits to clusters from a well-known foreign expert, most VMs did not have a happy experience with PRA as a means of discovering farmers' priorities and preferences, and doing participatory planning. One striking feature is that no diary noted refusals from villagers when the foreign expert was demonstrating PRA methods, but when the VMs tried to use them independently, villagers expressed opposition. The most likely explanation, given the empathy of VMs with villagers, is that villagers' cooperation with demonstration PRA exercises was at least partly based on the implicit authority of the foreign expert, which the VM lacked when seeking to use PRA independently. The VM of cluster A found that farmers in one hamlet blankly refused to cooperate with wealth-ranking (A, 15 December 1989); and the VM in cluster B expressed his problems with carrying out preference-ranking and social-mapping thus: 'When I ask them to think about themselves and to do preference ranking, social mapping, they get confused' (February 1992). He remarks that 'PRA is a long process. Here things doesn't come out very easily' (27 February 1992). What an 'expert' can do on the basis of implicit authority is not necessarily replicable by the VM.

If the authority of the VM was inadequate to engage villagers in PRA, it was also problematic within the management organisation. After eventually making his diagrams and maps and presenting them at a project planning workshop, the VM of cluster B returns to his village and notes that the PRA materials presented were not accepted and that 'the revision of the preference ranking [for agroforestry tree species] was essential'. He repeats the ranking, but gets the same result.

Furthermore, in this case, the outcome did not suggest that the methods had indeed uncovered preferences strong enough to sustain active involvement, for by 14 September 1992, when drought has hit cluster B, the VM finds farmers watering their papaya plants but not the sisoo, which are dying, and on enquiry he finds a lack of interest in sisoo, because timber is available in the forest and sisoo takes a long time to reach maturity. These species were, however, those chosen on the basis of preference-ranking. Supporters of PRA may argue that the ranking may have been done incorrectly. This is possible, but if a method cannot be reliably used by well-trained, highly motivated graduates, its usefulness is surely open to question. Later still, the diary shows the farmers failing to show up for nursery training, and it is difficult to escape the conclusion that incentives amount to more than sound preference-ranking, and that such ranking is not a definitive statement of a static and generalised preference.[5]

A series of diary entries in cluster A illustrates some of the problems and ironies of the VM situation. In cluster A, a sequence of diary entries records that farmers in meetings are repeatedly demanding irrigation in late 1989. Then the famous foreign PRA expert visits for a night (25 January 1990), followed by the VM going out and doing social-mapping and holding discussions with villagers in which 'problems were identified by tamarind seeds' (D, 26 January 1990). The irony of the vociferous villagers demanding irrigation, which the VM is unable to provide, given the poverty focus of the RFP, and the subsequent turn to divination by tamarind seed was not, I think, lost on the VM. The VM comments in the following days that he has visited the sites that the expert had visited and everywhere they asked him what had been the purpose of the visit. He explains. Villagers seemed puzzled and suspicious in the aftermath of the PRA. One can understand the puzzlement of those who, after clearly articulating what they saw as problems (lack of irrigation), are asked to play games with tamarind seeds to discover what the problems were. The

PRA here, arguably, both silences spontaneous demands and elicits at least a re-packaging within the vocabulary of participation, and at most a complete revision of 'local' priorities.

What much of the diary evidence suggests is that participation is understood as a discourse by villagers, a vocabulary which brings them into transactions with project staff, but from which they still seek material gain. For them participation is not an end in itself; it is the name of the game. Coming to meetings in order to get access to new seeds, or the food distributed at meetings, is one thing; sharing the time and information required by PRA, without any immediate return, is another. The VM as 'street level bureaucrat' experiences quite profound power-shifts which mean that his or her ability to carry through project objectives, or indeed to subvert them, is very dependent on context. Weakness and strength co-exist in quite contradictory ways, as the next section elaborates in looking at relations with other project staff and external organisations.

Field-worker relations within and between institutions

The VMs' legitimacy in village opinion depends to quite a large degree on their ability to command practical support from State institutions which are hierarchical, bureaucratic, and corrupt; to bring important visitors to their clusters; and to be seen as having a high status beyond the village. Yet they bear markers of low status in that external world — such as residence in a village, youth, or sometimes tribal origins. Similarly, within the project staff, although the CA and VM were considered a team, the reality was rather different. An indication is seen in the note in the cluster A diary following an ODA visit, when a Social Development Adviser asks what would happen in his cluster if he was not there. He notes his reply: that the CA could not cope, because 'the CA cannot do all the work. He cannot run after every plots' (A, 16 September 1990). Interestingly, he justifies his position in terms of being the person who actually visits and supervises the trials — a kind of assistant to the CA — not as a social analyst, not as a facilitator, or as the implementor of the non-agronomic project activities. This level of insecurity reflects the *de facto* relations between CA and VM, in which the cultural attributes of status (here age, caste, technical education, permanent employment) disempower the VM, the person who is at the front line.

VMs also have to manage the interface with other institutions, such as those of State rural development agencies, where they are at the front line in a clash of organisational styles. While the field-worker is relatively powerful in an informal and everyday sense, the external status of field-worker is quite low. The bureaucratic problems for a relatively low-status field-worker operating within the very structured and hierarchical work cultures of the Indian State, such as in trying to locate and obtain suitable seed, proved considerable. In Dantokhurd, the VM records a trip to Birsa University for this purpose in which he was kept waiting for four hours before being referred to three different departments, where he had to haggle (with only partial success) for seed, and was then sent to the university farm, where he waited for an hour — only to be told that the farm had closed and he should come back the next day. He spent the night in Ranchi and returned in the morning, but had to wait until the afternoon to be issued with the seed and then several more hours in order to pay (A, 4 October 1989).

Village residence results in friendships as well as less welcome obligations and demands. In cluster B, the VM found himself under considerable pressure to represent the villagers in approaching the BDO for a well. He tried to explain that this was not his job, but they insisted, pointing to his education and greater ability to command the attention of the BDO, an argument which proved hard to deny or resist. The social dynamics of power and patronage may help to deliver more apparent evidence of project achievements, but at the same time threaten longer-term sustainability, and possibly the danger of abuse of power. This is a dilemma confronted daily by VMs.

The VMs' relations with external consultants are described in their diaries.[6] One aspect of consultants' roles was that they directed the project back to a focus on poverty when the pressures in the village began seriously to undermine it.

Thus the experiments with seed-multiplication encountered disapproval from the consultants and ceased; and the consultants' continuing concern with identifying the socio-economic status of participants resulted in a visit which suggested the use of wealth-ranking to classify and monitor participating households (A, 5 December 1989). The VMs were always keen to respond to consultants' advice, even where it was problematic, as wealth-ranking was.

The activities in any one cluster, therefore, are a mixture of actors' preferences, including those of visiting consultants, in which the significance of farmers' preferences is difficult to gauge. For example, in cluster A, the move towards what was called agro-forestry emerged mainly from project managers and consultants; at cluster-level, meetings were held in March 1990 to discover 'farmers' choice' of trees. Following this, a meeting was held in April to plan a eucalyptus plantation — but no one attended. The VM discovered that on that day some of the people concerned had gone to their daily work and others had attended a meeting over the rape of a small girl by a 14-year old boy. The VM, however, continued to push agro-forestry and by early May was told by his superior that, before the imminent consultants' visit, 'agroforestry program is to be given stress and trial plot should be selected' (A, 3 May 1990). The VM still fails to get participant support and plaintively notes on 18 May 1991 that he is doing it 'I, myself, alone'. The VM is willing to substitute for the participants in order to cover the gap between the consultants' desires and the participants' resistance, rather than challenge the consultants, or reveal the absence of participation. Where interlocking projects cannot be constructed, the VM shoulders the burden.

The question of whom the consultants choose to speak to has been raised in connection with field-worker discretion; it is also an issue with participants, who frequently make comments and criticisms to VMs about being excluded. Participants also clearly saw high visibility to consultants as a favour dispensed by the VM (with the possibility of resources following in the wake of consultants' visits), and complaints were made when certain hamlets, often the less accessible, felt left out (C, 23 September 1991). A greater problem for consultants to overcome is the degree to which the relationship between field-worker and participants makes it difficult to hold critical discussions about the project with villagers, who tend to close ranks with project staff, understanding the possible consequences of perceived project failure. Participants and field-staff collude in representing success.

As far as status is concerned, there are contradictory demands in the field-worker role: low to minimise the social distance from villages and facilitate participation, but high in order to have effective relations outside the village; formally equal to the technical staff, but informally inferior to them. In addition, the pressures towards patronage within the social dynamics of the village, but against it in project objectives, are real problems in the lived experience of field-workers — but largely unrecognised in project planning and management.

Conclusions

The field-workers' diaries were an inspired suggestion and offer unusual insights into the making of a project in a specific local context. They provide, in long-term projects such as RFP, a valuable opportunity to study interactive change during the course of a development intervention. Some of the lessons learned from their analysis derive from an understanding of the social positioning of the village-based field-worker, and others are gained from the view of the field-worker as a subject interactively constructing the project around his or her own understandings and villagers' own 'projects', rather than as a project 'implementor'.

The diaries show that it takes time to establish meaningful contact with poor villagers, and this process cannot be accelerated. It is not the case that a model of participation can be evolved in one place and then applied elsewhere much more quickly, and the implication for the expansion of the RFP is that movement to new areas may well need as much time as the work in the original clusters. Understanding the complexities of power and patronage in field-worker experience indicates potential problems in the notion of a catalytic project, igniting participatory develop-

ment and moving on to new areas. There are also conflicting tensions between the pressures on the VM towards a benign relationship of patronage, in which the VM is recognised and valued by local people, and the needs of the project for the development of sustainable institutions, in which project staff are dispensable, in advance of the withdrawal of the project. As a participatory mechanism, PRA can, ironically, be difficult to conduct where field-workers are not in a position of authority. Finally, consultants have been, and will continue to be, important actors in the shaping of RFP in indirect ways, of which they will usually be unaware and to which there needs to be greater sensitivity.

When the subjectivity of field-workers is addressed, a less innocent view of participation follows from the insight that farmers and field-workers are engaged in a process of mutual enrolment in their interactions; farmers readily learn the language of participation, and what is articulated should not too readily be taken, at face value, as a thoroughgoing adherence to participatory philosophies. Participants and field-workers collude in representing project success to 'outsiders', be they HQ staff, evaluators contracted by donors, local or foreign consultants; this is rarely taken into account, but is important to both evaluations and the working understanding of the project by all non-field-staff.

As well as offering some observations on the character of the RFP, I hope this paper has made a convincing case that we should conceive of *both* field-workers and participants as active agents, interacting at the critical social interface, and trying to find common ground between project objectives and villagers' aspirations and desires. Project managers, funders, and consultants can learn a great deal from a better understanding of the struggles of field-workers at the sharp end, recognition of which is long overdue.

Notes

1 I thank the following people for helpful comments on the draft of this paper: Ros Eyben, Mike Wilson, Richard Palmer-Jones, Sarah Ladbury, Ian Carruthers, Alan Rew, and Steve Jones. This paper is based on two visits to the project, firstly in the Phase 2 preparation mission, which visited project staff in all three States and included time spent with staff in their clusters, and then later when I spent several weeks researching, with project field-staff, three cluster histories in 1994–5. I am grateful for the assistance of PK Mukherjee, Mr Phani and all the project staff at RFP. Above all else this paper is a tribute to the VMs of the RFP.

2   Of course, the VM view is only one perspective: other important actors were the Indian management organisation, the Hindustani Fertiliser Corporation (HFC), the funders, Overseas Development Administration (ODA), and the UK consultants, Overseas Development Group (ODG). A secondary stakeholder analysis of the different visions and the interactions of these organisations would greatly add to the completeness of the story, but is beyond the scope of the paper.

3   For an interesting comparison, see David Mosse's paper on KRIBP in western India (1995).

4   Village Level Worker, i.e. an extension agent.

5   In cluster A the VM had a similarly disheartening experience. At one ODA visit the team ask him about how the tree species are chosen, and the VM replies 'by preference ranking' (A, 20 September 1991). But still there is much reluctance, and on 31 March 1992 he writes that he "met Mohan X about the sisoo and eucalyptus plantation. I told him he has to do nursery for which he told that he is poor so he cannot look after the nursery since he has to go for work.' On 11 May the VM held a meeting for 'motivation for nursery raising', because of the lack of support, and at the meeting the farmers said that it takes much labour and that since they are not paid they cannot do it.

6   Farmers' comments recorded in the diary reveal something of the mystery surrounding the visitations of consultants and ODA; in 1990 the VM of cluster A notes that the farmers observe that ODA representatives always come before and after harvest, but not during it. It is as if villagers carefully observe the behaviour of consultants and try to make sense of it; they search for clues in, say, the timing of visits, but remain rather mystified. Consultants were seldom aware of the extent to which villagers were prepared by the VM for their visits, anxious about the out-come of visits, speculative of the deep meanings behind any changes in the timing or details of the visit programme and clamorous for feedback after the visits.

References

Booth, D. (1994) (ed) *Rethinking Social Development: Theory, Research and Practice*, London: Longman.

Clay, E. and B. Schaffer (eds) (1984) *Room for Manoeuvre* London: Heinemann.

Goetz, A.M. (1996) 'Local Heroes: Patterns of Fieldworker Discretion in Implementing GAD Policy in Bangladesh', Institute of Development Studies Discussion Paper 358.

Giddens, A. (1984) *The Constitution of Society: an Outline of the Theory of Structuration*, Cambridge: Polity Press.

Jackson, C. (1997) 'Actor orientation and gender relations at a participatory project interface' in A. M. Goetz (ed): *Breaking in: Speaking out: Getting Institutions Right for Women in Development*, London: Zed Press (forthcoming).

Lipsky, M. (1980) *Street-level Bureaucracy: Dilemmas of the Individual in Public Service*, New York: Russel Sage.

Long, N. and N. Long (eds) (1992) *Battlefields of Knowledge: the Interlocking of Theory and Practice in Social Research and Development*, London: Routledge.

Mosse, D. (1995) 'People's knowledge in project planning: the limits and social conditions of participation in planning agricultural development', Overseas Development Institute, Agricultural Research and Development Network Paper 58.

Overseas Development Group (ODG) (1995) 'Handover report from ODG to ODA, covering the period April 1989–March 1995', University of East Anglia: Norwich.

Wade, R. (1992) 'How to make "street-level bureaucracies" work better: India and Korea', *Institute of Development Studies Bulletin* 43 (4), 51–4.

The author

Cecile Jackson is a Lecturer at the School of Development Studies at the University of East Anglia. This article first appeared in *Development in Practice*, Volume 7, Number 3, in 1997.

North–South relations and the question of aid

Mustafa Barghouthi

The North–South dynamic and national boundaries

The North–South divide is socio-economic and political, rather than geographical. Firstly, the so-called North itself suffers from a multitude of internal social and economic problems. Indeed, many countries in the North are experiencing internal North–South tensions.

Secondly, millions of people from the South now live within the geographical boundaries of the North. Even so, they remain part of the South and, as such, suffer great discrimination in Germany, Britain, France, and Italy, and elsewhere.

Thirdly, the collapse of the Soviet Union has demonstrated that many Eastern European nations are in fact so under-developed that they could easily be classified as 'Southern' countries.

However, there are also divisions within the South itself. Already, the South is experiencing the 'centre versus periphery' phenomenon. There are also divisions resulting in part of the North in fact living in the South. In the Middle East, for example, Israel belongs in economic terms to the North, while the Occupied Territories are definitely part of the South.

Finally, this is a period of transition worldwide, mainly in the economic sphere. As an adviser to the US President recently expressed it, in the future there will 'no longer be national products or technologies, no national corporations or industries. All that will remain rooted are people that comprise a nation.'

What was not stated is that within each nation there are, and will continue to be, more national divisions. Similarly ignored is the fact that common interests are emerging, uniting people across national boundaries. The globalisation of issues such as the environment highlights one of the most important aspects of North–South dynamics: their interdependence. This factor is impossible to ignore, whether the subject is the ozone problem or AIDS. The nuclear accident at Chernobyl is just one example of an environmental disaster and resulting health problems which are not confined to the boundaries of one particular nation.

Economic exploitation also crosses national boundaries. Much of what will happen in the future depends on the level of skilled human resources available in each country: the continuing 'brain drain' from the South to the North demonstrates that the industrial countries are exploiting the ever-widening economic gap to attract the most active and educated people from the South. This in turn strengthens the factors which gave rise to the gap, and ensures that it is sustained in the future.

The gap is universal, with economic, social, political, and health dimensions. As a result, developing-world debt and economic aid are now instruments to control the economies of the South, to keep developing countries in a situation where their markets, resources, and raw materials will always be available to serve the interests of the general capital market.

Quantitative v. qualitative analysis

Any evaluation of the situation in Southern or developing countries must be based on more than conventional quantitative analysis. In the field of health, for example, it is not sufficient to measure the infant mortality rate or life expectancy, while ignoring the questions of quality of life, and social justice for people in developing countries. Inequality is evident even in terms of the consumption patterns imposed on Southern countries. Many industrial countries export second-rate materials and goods to the South. Moreover, it is evident that second-rate development standards are being used. The question of quality must be central to the evaluation of North–South relations.

Aid money and North–South relationships

The first question is whether it is truly possible to establish relations on an equal footing between a funder and a recipient. Can one honestly speak of partnerships in this context? Over the last decade, governments have become the major source of aid funding, and the vast majority of development money takes the form of bilateral government-to-government support. Northern NGOs are increasingly dependent on their governments for funds, and this in turn has resulted in a clear change in the policies of these organisations. The level of professionalism within development aid organisations is such that one could even speak of the 'aid business' in the North. The result is that some of these are, in effect, forcing recipient NGOs to follow along behind them, thus making them too dependent on the government aid they receive. USAID funding is an example: its operation has always been political. However, the question is whether this aid, or most of it, is actually being used in order to develop Southern countries, or whether it is being used primarily to benefit the economy of the North. It is worth examining, for example, how much of the money is used to purchase military equipment or goods that are compatible with Western consumption patterns and serve Western marketing needs.

The allocation of funds

The question here is: who determines funding priorities? Most often — and the Occupied Territories are a case in point — funders arrive without clearly defined plans or strategy, only a 'charitable' mind-set. Generally, priorities are decided by the funders and not the recipients, which accounts for the emphasis on purchasing equipment. For example, the EC requires in most cases that a substantial portion of its support be used to purchase equipment and, moreover, that this should be from the countries providing the funding. Is all this equipment really necessary? If huge sums of money are provided for infrastructural costs, what happens in the future if we fail to get the resources necessary to cover maintenance or running costs? The contradiction here, or rather the question to which no one has supplied an answer, is how 'self-reliance' and 'sustainability' can be achieved when the bulk of funds is being spent on equipment and machines, rather than human resources.

Training and technical expertise

Another aspect is the question of training, currently a popular trend among funders. If huge numbers of people in the South are trained, but the facilities or money necessary to employ them are not available, eventually they will either leave for the North or be unemployed. The value of training programmes must be questioned, if they are not clearly linked to provision of running costs or job opportunities.

Furthermore, while there is a great need in many developing countries for technical expertise, it should come not only from the North but also from the South. There is no reason why experts from India cannot be sent to advise certain programmes in the Occupied Territories, or why a Mexican health project cannot benefit from a Palestinian consultant. The flow of expertise need not always be North to South — a point even more relevant in terms of cost-effectiveness, when the cost of technical experts from the North is ten to fifteen times higher than those from the South.

Fashions in funding

Another problem affecting the relationship between Northern and Southern organisations is the constantly shifting priorities of Northern NGOs and governments, to follow the latest trends in development. Such shifts have a distinct negative impact on programmes in the recipient countries, as in one institution which had initiated a child-health project. The issue of child health was attractive to funders at the time, and the project was supported. However, the following year the funding agency announced that its new programme was to be maternal and child health, so the institution was forced to alter its project to fit in with this concept. The third year the trend turned to women's health, and the institution had to change its project once again to suit the target interest. Such a situation distorts the recipient organisation's objectives and introduces moral distortion, in that the recipients find themselves forced either to cheat in their representations to the funders, or change their programme at the expense of their own priorities.

In addition, the majority of funders insist that funding should not exceed a period of one to three years. There are exceptions — some organisations have been involved in long-term development work for many years and have a different philosophy — but the majority set short-term funding conditions which call into question the possibility of achieving real development. Sometimes a project may need at least one to two years to get on a firm footing and, if the funding is to last only another year, real sustainability is threatened. Yet sustainability is the watchword constantly presented to recipient organisations.

Is sustainability a valid concept when aid is given in small portions, as in the Occupied Territories? In 1992, western Germany poured funds into eastern Germany equivalent to the entire amount of aid that was given to developing countries. In one country of 16 million people, the amount of foreign aid money was the same as that going to the rest of the world, from all countries, not merely from Germany. This suggests that serious development cannot be achieved by small sums given here and there. Major structural changes are required before true development, aimed at self-reliance and self-sufficiency, can be realised.

Moreover, while recognising the value of concepts such as self-reliance and sustainability, a health organisation, if it operates in an occupied country, does not have a government which could raise taxes and subsidise the health system, and so it must be subsidised if it is to reach those most in need. An endowment would seem to be the answer, because it would allow the gradual build-up of self-reliance. However, with very few exceptions, no funding organisation is willing to accept the idea of an endowment. The reason generally given is that with an endowment the funding organisation has no guarantee that the character of the recipient organisation will not change over time. However, organisations in the North receive endowment funds, despite the fact that their character may also change. It would seem more equitable to apply the same standards in the South as in the North in this respect.

The administrative burden

A common requirement is that administrative costs should be kept to a minimum, which is fair. Ideally, administrative work should be done on a voluntary basis, because this helps a grassroots organisation retain its character and integrity. However, when donors require detailed narrative and financial reports every six months as well as audited financial reports, they are in fact pushing recipient organisations towards bureaucratisation, forcing an expansion in the administrative structure in order to handle their demands. In the Occupied Territories, numerous grassroots organisations have been forced in the direction of institutionalisation and at that point, many of them lose forever their grassroots character.

Monitoring and evaluation

Evaluations pose yet another challenge to an open and fair relationship between funding and recipient organisations. Evaluations are almost always commissioned by the funders — those providing the money. Furthermore, some donor agencies choose to send an evaluation mission of two or three people from the funding country to evaluate a programme and try to find solutions to problems that recipient countries or organisations may have spent years working out. Never has the evaluation process been reversed, with a Southern organisation travelling North to evaluate the work of a funder. The organisations in the South are the primary beneficiaries of the funding process, as well as being the ones doing the bulk of the work on the ground. Shouldn't these be the ones to evaluate development programmes and judge their success or failure?

Apolitical advocacy

Finally, there is the widely held view that development aid must be apolitical and, usually, based on the concept of charity. When it comes to advocacy on difficult questions such as the Palestinian–Israeli issue, most organisations become 'apolitical'. When the USSR collapsed, however, most funding went to eastern Europe. This was a political decision. In development, clearly, any avowedly apolitical move is actually profoundly political. This is especially clear when one remembers that little development can be achieved in the absence of democracy.

Prospects for the future of the relationship

The first step on the road to changing some aspects of the process of funding development is for Southern organisations to be united in their stand, and to engage in dialogue with Northern organisations. This should, ideally, have an influence on policy decisions, which would allow changes to occur. However, the objective is not to form an alliance of Southern organisations opposing those in the North, but instead to aim for the establishment of a trans-geographical coalition of people who believe in social justice, equity, and democracy, in order to influence the process. Secondly, Southern organisations should determine priorities, rather than organisations from outside, and funders should be required to provide long-term commitments. Thirdly, development should aim to be a democratic process, and it should be true, sustainable

development rather than mere cosmetic changes.

Steps to close the huge economic gap between North and South are essential, since real change is impossible without them. Unless the Third World debt is cancelled, the global economy cannot be corrected.

Major emphasis should be placed on human resources, specifically on skills. If the Northern countries were to divert 50 per cent of what they spend on arms alone, these funds would be sufficient to institute honest development programmes that could start the process of closing the economic gap between countries of South and North.

At a practical level, this should be possible even in the current international situation, primarily because of interdependence and the globalisation of issues discussed earlier. Any environmental problems in the South will, for example, affect the North — and there will be a growing number of interested groups in the North which will fight for change. What is needed is a clear vision, clear strategy, clear policies, and lots of creativity. Similarly, the organisations within developing countries must be self-critical, open-minded, and flexible.

Finally, one of the biggest challenges facing grassroots movements and organisations in the South is to understand the huge changes that have occurred in the world. Whether they seem desirable or not, they must be fully understood before changes can be made and the slogans such as 'Health for All' can become an instrument of real change in a world that has never been so powerful, and yet has never been so confused in its efforts to find the right path towards the future.

The author

Dr Mustafa Barghouthi is a founder member of the Union of Palestine Medical Relief Committees, a voluntary movement with a membership of over 1,000 health professionals in the West Bank and Gaza Strip. At the time of writing he was the first president of the International People's Health Council, founded in 1991. This article first appeared in *Development in Practice*, Volume 3, Number 3, in 1993.

Collaboration with the South:
agents of aid or solidarity?

Firoze Manji

Like other donor countries, the United Kingdom has been channelling a significant proportion of its development aid through non-government organisations (NGOs). In a review of the effectiveness of this form of aid, several studies have been commissioned by the UK Overseas Development Administration (ODA), the latest of which focused on exploring UK development NGOs' attitudes to increasing the proportion of aid channelled by the ODA directly to Southern NGOs (Bebbington and Riddell, 1995). Based on a questionnaire survey, this study provides an intriguing insight into the British NGO (BINGO) psyche. It suggests that, despite years of interactions with the Third World, there remains a considerable deficit of respect and trust for their counterparts in the South.

According to the survey, most (80 per cent) of BINGOs are *opposed* to aid being channelled directly to Southern NGOs, for a number of reasons. They allege that Southern NGOs

- lack the experience to undertake rigorous monitoring and evaluation of projects;
- lack experience of how to manage projects in accordance with donors' requirements;
- with direct funding, would shift their accountability away from their own constituencies towards donor agencies;
- would become more directly influenced by donor agencies in setting their agenda, and hence more 'donor-driven';
- would eventually respond to the availability of money rather than the meeting of needs;

- would eventually fill a void created by a retrenching State;
- would be susceptible to manipulation by donor agencies, and more susceptible to political influence.

In addition, they argue, there would be a loss of the 'neutrality' provided by BINGOs; and it would be cheaper to fund projects in the South via BINGOs.

What is striking about this list of reasons against direct funding of Southern NGOs is that, were logic to prevail, most Northern NGOs would not qualify either to receive funds from ODA. Are these features really the exclusive property of Southern NGOs? To what extent are they shared by their Northern counterparts?

In my experience, very few NGOs — either in the North or the South — can with all honesty claim always to monitor, manage, and evaluate their projects adequately. Poor management has been the bane of many projects, something that is increasingly recognised, if attendance rates at project-management training courses are anything to go by. Most experienced development NGOs would probably agree that monitoring and evaluation could be improved, and even long-established BINGOs are often criticised for not managing their projects in accordance with the donors' requirements.

What about accountability? Most BINGOs are non-membership organisations. As such, they are rarely accountable to anyone other than a self-appointed Board. In most cases, even those who contribute regularly to the organisation have no rights to determine its policy or to elect its Trustees. In almost every case, their constituency — understood to mean either those who benefit from the projects, or the Southern NGOs — has no rights to determine a BINGO's policy or practice. So how accountable are they? Certainly, they are required to be accountable 'upwards' to their donors, an accountability for which there are both structural mechanisms and rights embodied in the grant documents (if not in law). But such mechanisms are seldom accorded to their Southern partners (or their beneficiaries). Would it not be fair to say that, for most BINGOs, accountability has long ago shifted away from their constituencies towards the donor agencies? Have BINGOs not been interested in establishing structural mechanisms that would increase, over time, the degree to which they became accountable to their Southern counterparts? How many BINGOs have, for example, representatives of their Southern counterpart organisations on their Board of Trustees? That this is more the exception than the rule speaks volumes about their concern for ensuring their own 'downward' accountability.

Can BINGOs really claim to be immune from the influence of donor agencies? Are they not guilty not only of being driven by these but also, in turn, of setting and influencing the agenda of their Southern counterparts — with whom, let us be clear, they have a donor–recipient relationship? Looking at the projects and programmes in which BINGOs have been involved over the last three decades, it is clear that the focus of their activity shifts with the trends and fancies of the donors, to the extent that project proposals and reports mimic the latest jargon ('sustainable development', 'civil society' and so on) on which ODA has decided to focus. When donor agencies hold the money, is it surprising that NGOs are prone to being driven by their agenda?

Do BINGOs always respond to need, rather than to the source of potential funding? Looking at the proportion of ODA's funds which have moved from the poorest parts of the world towards Eastern Europe and the former Soviet Union, a shift equally reflected in the funding profiles of many NGOs, many observers might feel that need tends to be a neglected parameter for determining priorities. Where is the justification for the claim that BINGOs are any more likely than Southern NGOs to respond to needs rather than chasing after money?

As for filling the void of a retrenching State, one needs only look at the British indigenous NGO scene over the last decade. As successive governments have clawed back social expenditure, numerous charities have ardently rushed to fill the vacuum. Is there any evidence that Southern NGOs are any more prone to this tendency than their British counterparts?

Claims that British NGOs are somehow more 'neutral' than Southern ones are hard to take seriously, and suggest a depth of paternalism that is surprising to find so late in the twentieth century. Like their missionary precursors 100 years ago, British NGOs have for years played, and continue to play, a less than neutral role with respect to the interests of British foreign policy, of which overseas aid is not an insignificant part. BINGOs have their own biases and prejudices, as this survey clearly demonstrates. Just because these prejudices are so widely held does not mean that they should be taken to represent a form of neutrality. If BINGOs tend to be neutral, it may frequently be in relation to the less than benign role of British imperial policies.

The arguments advanced by British NGOs against direct funding hide a more profound discomfort. I believe that this may be an expression of the primordial fear among some BINGOs that if donor agencies start funding Southern organisations directly, then their own future is at risk. It is the *cri du coeur* of the dinosaur facing potential extinction. It is tempting to draw the conclusion that the *raison d'être* for development may no longer be to build sustainable development and institutions in the South, but rather to keep the home team going. Direct funding of Southern NGOs represents a direct threat to the survival of Northern NGOs in their present form. What we need is a discussion about the future role of Northern NGOs in an era where Southern NGOs are fully able — at least to the same degree as BINGOs — to manage funds provided directly to them by donors.

Are there not also good reasons to question the commitment, capacity, and willingness of

British NGOs to 'build capacity' in the South? The results of this survey suggest that, after more than 50 years of 'development', British NGOs feel that they have signally failed to build viable, independent, sustainable Southern institutions which are capable of managing donor agencies' attempts to manipulate them, can run programmes effectively, and carry out rigorous monitoring and evaluation. If this is so, what exactly has been the purpose of their activities over the last few decades? Are we to assume that pronouncing a commitment to 'sustainable development' and institutional capacity-building is just public relations for the benefit of the 'punter' whose contributions are being sought?

But this raises a serious issue: is it feasible for an organisation to be effective in institutional capacity-building if, at the same time, its relationship with its Southern counterpart is mediated through money? From the perspective of most Southern NGOs, there may be, in effect, little difference between dealing with ODA and dealing with a Northern NGO, since in both cases the relationship is one of donor–recipient. No matter how sympathetic the donor may be, nor how good the personal relations between them, the fact that the Northern NGO is the one with the money means that the Southern NGO must be the one with the begging bowl. Perforce, there is a relationship of unequals. And inequality never built capacity. It nurtures dependence. It establishes the material basis for dancing to the tune of the donor.

My purpose here is not to argue the case for or against direct funding of Southern NGOs by ODA. But I am deeply uneasy about the underlying motives of BINGOs that lead them to oppose such funding. Perhaps even more disturbing is the lack of critical assessment of ODA policies, especially in assessing the extent to which BINGOs are themselves being used by the British State in the same way that they fear Southern NGOs might be used if the money were channelled to them directly. After more than 500 years at the receiving end of British goodwill in Africa and elsewhere in the South, a period characterised by pillage, slavery, genocide, colonisation, and more recently a develop-ment paradigm that results in more wealth flowing from the South to the North than the other way around (aid budgets notwithstanding) — to say nothing of the support and arms provided to despots — one would have thought that a healthy scepticism about UK foreign policy and development aid would be the norm. Perhaps BINGOs should be looking at how they themselves might be being used and manipulated by donor funds, just as they so perspicaciously highlight the risks faced by Southern NGOs.

What we need today is a greater reflection by Northern NGOs on the nature of their relationship with their Southern counterparts. If we are seriously committed to the struggle to eliminate poverty and injustice and their causes, we need to assess the degree to which the nature of that relationship may be hampering rather than enhancing our common goals; to examine how to build alliances with Southern NGOs that are based on solidarity, not charity; and to look at whether we are being used, albeit unconsciously, by aid agencies to achieve ends that subvert rather than promote those values we hold dear. We need to question whether the overall effect of British aid has indeed led to improving the conditions of the poor in the South, and, if not, after all these years of trying, to ask why. We must explore ways for us to be as accountable to our Southern partners as we expect them to be to us. And we need to break away from the tradition of paternalism which has been so lucidly revealed in the recent study. To do otherwise is to risk becoming the agents of aid.

References

Bebbington, A and R. Riddell (1995), *Donors, Civil Society and Southern NGOs: New Agendas, Old Problems*, London: IIED/ODA.

The author

Firoze Manji has been Director of Amnesty International's Africa Programme and Chief Executive Officer of the Aga Khan Foundation (UK). This article first appeared in *Development in Practice* Volume 7, Number 3, in 1997.

Partners and beneficiaries:
questioning donors

Richard Moseley-Williams

Introduction

How, and through whom, should Northern development-funding NGOs like Oxfam (UK and Ireland) direct their funds and seek to achieve their goals in the South? The first part of this article[1] discusses the intermediaries between donor and beneficiary: the Southern NGOs and other groups and institutions — we tend to call them *partners* or, with fewer connotations of cohabitation, *counterparts* — who are the recipients of grants and who carry responsibility for delivering the project to the intended population. The assertion is that in the pursuit of their strategic objectives, donors like Oxfam will increasingly look more widely for intermediaries, including and beyond the Southern NGOs of the 1980s; and that clearer criteria are needed to help to decide who are — and who are not — the right holders of grants for development projects. At the same time, as the role of Southern NGOs has changed, so has the Northern donor context; and agencies like Oxfam now have to reconcile pressures and priorities in which Southern partners' interests figure less prominently than before.

Why do we need intermediaries? The intention of the second part of this article is to prove the value of partners — but also to challenge donors to demonstrate that *they* are adding as much value as possible to the relationship between donor, intermediary, and beneficiary. The suggested conclusion is that the principal contribution of donors such as Oxfam should be in the more imaginative use of their 'comparative advantages', among which are (relatively) large and (relatively) untied grants budgets; in many cases radical, non-partisan traditions, and the power to resist the blandishments of public opinion and the pressure of vested interests; and, for the larger, longer-established donors, the accumulated experience of decades of development work in non-industrialised countries.

Northern funding for NGO partners is much affected by the way in which Southern NGOs vary, according to their many different national contexts and histories. In Latin America, some factors which influenced the growth of European-style NGOs were the early history of European colonisation, followed by over a century and a half of independence. In Southern Africa, most national NGOs were created more recently: in many cases as counterparts of Northern NGOs whose constitutions they adapted; in others, as structures born in struggle for independence and majority rule. Like the newly independent republics, it is only now that many African NGOs are in the process of redefining their social and political role. The African experience has more to do with anti-colonialism, anti-racism, and nation-building, whereas Latin American NGOs were influenced more by class, anti-militarism, and anti-US feeling. In both regions, however, many of today's NGOs grew up in the decades after the 1960s, representing civil society excluded from representation in the

State and in the socio-economic structures which dominated the political process. The relatively strong NGO movements which emerged are generally quite different from what came out of one-party statist post-colonial societies in West and Central/East Africa; and different again from the expressions of civil society in the strife-torn countries of the Horn.

Varieties of NGOs and other potential intermediaries

There is an enormous number and variety of philanthropic non-government groups in most of the countries where Northern funders deliver their assistance. In England and Wales alone, there are no fewer than 170,000 registered charities. If Brazil or South Africa or Argentina or Nigeria had laws which gave the concessions and status allowed under UK charity law, they would probably have proportionately as many registered organisations. Mexico is said to have 30,000 non-profit-making *asociaciones civiles*. In India, the number of non-profit organisations is enormous. Smaller states like Bolivia or Haiti or Zambia or Senegal also have registered NGOs of many kinds. And, in all countries, vast numbers of social groupings exist besides those recognised by the law. Of course they do; here we see the innumerable family, community, interest, and religious structures which give society its form and variety. So, while they may have strategic significance beyond their numbers, the partners of donor NGOs can be only a tiny and selected part of a wider 'civil society'. This fact immediately puts into perspective the potential of Southern NGOs to effect wider social and political change.

Many non-formal groups are or could be our partners. There is, for instance, no obligation on Oxfam to channel funds through legally constituted bodies, provided that accountability is assured (and Oxfam's experience suggests that there is no close correlation between legal status and good reporting). If Oxfam had as its object the improvement of the health of poor people in a hypothetical village or city slum, and this was best pursued by channelling a grant through (for

the sake of argument) an unrecognised circle of traditional healers or general practitioners — rather than the local elite of trained medical professionals recognised by the official health service — then Oxfam might well have *a legal obligation* under its UK charitable status to try to support the former, no matter how much better would be the reporting from the latter.

The same applies to partnership with structures within the State. State ministries or local government structures appear on Oxfam grants lists as partners. Yet one detects some reluctance to confess the relationship, as if something shameful or incompatible was involved. This embarrassment may be felt on both sides. High-level civil servants and their political masters may see NGOs as threatening, unprofessional, and irrelevant; NGOs may think of civil servants and politicians as overpaid parasites and rule-bound time-servers of the *status quo*. The truth is that there is variety in the State as there is among the NGOs. With the withering away of the totalitarian State, greater political pluralism in many formerly hard-line regimes, and increasing abandonment by governments of their monopoly of welfare provision, the opportunities have increased for donors to use their influence and funding levers effectively to work with more progressive groups within civil services. This can be done cautiously and strategically, so there need be no compromise of cherished NGO principles and the social basis of support.

The choice of intermediary

Having established the wide range of potential intermediaries or partners, the question is: how are they chosen by the funding agencies? The official answer will be that, strictly speaking, the intermediary is selected as the group most likely to deliver the project. In practice, partners are approached because of this — but also because they broadly mirror the funder's development philosophy.[2] Donor agencies with religious motives will seek out partners through networks like the World Council of Churches, CIDSE, and the Islamic groups; political organisations will operate through ideological connections such as those linked to German Christian Democrat funding, USAID, or the former Soviet sphere of influence. Like other donors, Oxfam tends to gravitate towards those which are closest to its policies and style.

What are the criteria for choice? For Oxfam and like-minded agencies, the three main ones are the following:

- effective, accountable option for the poor and social base among the poor;
- commitment to empowerment; and
- styles of working which reflect professed commitment.

Option for the poor and social base among the poor

This criterion means that the intermediary must have a proven commitment to the cause of the poor and to effective delivery of projects to them; there must be ways in which the partner can be called to account by the intended beneficiaries; and there must be evidence of a basis of grassroots support for the intervention concerned. In the moral and practical sense, the project holder — whether this is a tiny community group or a large government department — must be 'on the side' of the poor.

Commitment to empowerment

The idea of basing development on a process of acquiring power has led to the creation of a specialised lexicon (*self-help; self-sufficiency; conscientisation; participation;* and today's developmentally correct word, *sustainability*). None of these is as useful in encapsulating what we mean as Oxfam's twenty-year old 'mission statement' ('Oxfam: An Interpretation') where development was defined as 'to have and to be more'. 'Being more' captures the notion of social power acquired (not power given over or handed down by others), as well as a psychological element of self-respect and confidence.

Whatever word we use, we must allow for this 'having and being more'. We must ask questions of 'sustainability': an ugly word which correctly captures the importance to development of self-sufficiency and continuity, but which, used

loosely and without qualification (sustainable development?), can be used to justify little change to the *status quo*. You can be sustained in wretched poverty, ignorance, and oppression, like some medieval serf. Subsistence agriculture is 'sustainable', but is it developmental? One suspects that the poor would understand 'sustainability' as the language of the *haves* rather than the *have nots*.

Work styles reflecting professed commitment

There is no doubt that donors' choice of partner (and partners' choice of donor) is influenced by attitudes and organisational procedures with which we feel comfortable. Top-down, high-salary, masculine, nine-to-five, vehicle-heavy organisations fare less well in grant recommendations from field staff than groups which are more democratic, hard-working, tightly budgeted, and take the bus. There is of course a large measure of hypocrisy often present here. But above and beyond the double standards is a legitimate point about styles of work appropriate to those — in donor agencies as well as in partner organisations — who engage with the poor in the fight against poverty and injustice. It is legitimate for donors to ask these questions of partners — though we must be prepared to have the same questions asked of ourselves.

A potential danger

The above arguments are not to deny the importance of long-term relationships between donors and counterparts or partners, but only to point out that donors are increasingly playing a more active and flexible role *in addition* to maintaining these relationships, where they work effectively.

What has also changed is the philosophy which regarded the growth of national NGOs as 'a good thing' because it was to do with the emergence of popular movements representing the poor. Experience has shown that, while some NGOs emerged and managed to remain as expressions of the poor at times of rapid change, many others lined up more with the dominant classes. The phenomenon of NGOs becoming capital-city havens of sheltered employment for bureaucrats retrenched by political change or structural adjustment is widely and rightly criticised in Africa, Latin America, and elsewhere. In some critical situations, NGOs have paid better salaries, often in hard currency, and so attracted scarce and greatly needed skills away from weakened public services.

Having said this, there is the danger of giving Southern development NGOs a uniformly bad press. The fact is that countries have different experiences. One hears some NGOs criticised in Peru or Uganda or Mozambique; whereas in El Salvador or Brazil or Zimbabwe some are, or have been, important development actors. Nor must one forget that most of the most successful and meaningful project work and issue work which Oxfam and other funders have supported has been in partnership with, and largely dependent on, courageous and visionary Southern NGOs. These are not alone in struggling to come to terms with the development crisis of the 1990s. The process of marginalisation and impoverishment of a large part of the population of the planet is one in which we are all involved. Northern donors must also face up to new challenges — and our Southern counterparts probably perform no better and no worse than we do.

However, Southern NGO contributions to South–North coalition-building, to regional initiatives in the ACP world, and to Southern contributions to the development debate, are sadly unrecognised. It is as if the South is seen as a passive recipient of micro-projects, while policy debates and lobbying efforts are concentrated in the North. The argument for Northern lobbying is that this reflects where the important decisions have come to lie, especially after the Cold War. This is a flawed analysis, not only because Southerners do not want or need Northerners to decide things for them. It also neglects the key question: Where is political power in the arena of global poverty generated? The answer, of course, is in the South. Without Southern pressure, Northern governments and opposition parties would pay little attention to the needs of the poor world, beyond a general recognition of the need to provide relief aid. This pressure is also important for funding NGOs in the North, both in making the public more aware of Southern issues and in agencies' internal debates about priorities.

We must therefore recognise the significance of key Southern NGOs; and we should guard against playing into the hands of the enemies of development who would be delighted to see Northern donors undermine their counterparts in the South. But we need to distinguish between NGOs; and avoid the catch-all notion of an NGO 'movement', such as was understood in the 1980s. In the same vein, we must be careful not to accept uncritically generalisations such as the alleged link between NGOs and the strength of 'civil society'. Again, the issue is what the NGO stands for — and there is an enormous variety.

'Going operational'

Critics will rightly point to the thin line that exists between a more active development-support role by donors, and the assumption of operational or management responsibility for projects, by-passing partners' structures. Here again, there has been a change in what used to be an article of faith. A decade ago 'self-help and non-interference' philosophies subscribed to by Oxfam and others renounced a 'hands-on' approach by field staff. The aim was to accompany the project holder, providing support but guarding against interfering or imposing, wittingly or unwittingly, our dubious Northern values. This line of thinking sounds today a little patronising and old-fashioned. We are now more pragmatic and tend to allow relationships with partners to find their own levels.

Do we need partners at all? We donors do, most emphatically. There is no more effective way in which we could deliver our aid and keep faith with our empowerment brief. Our partners are on the whole better than we at identifying need, obtaining the support of the beneficiary community, designing project proposals, managing and evaluating projects, and engaging in development debate. Where there is no partner, our instinct is to create an intermediary to take over the project.

The question whether we need development partners would have been thought absurd in Oxfam until a few years ago. Today, however, there are forces pushing in the direction of greater operationality — and these may become stronger in the future. They come from various places: from fundraising needs, where it is easier to appeal for public support for 'Oxfam projects' which can be suitably dressed up without upsetting partners' sensitivities; from increasing stress within agencies on planning, objective-setting, and performance-measurement, which partners facing rapid change will find difficulty in accommodating; from the relative success in income terms of the 'operational' agencies like ActionAid and World Vision; from the ODA, the European Union, and other government donors who would be happy to channel more funds through us Northern NGOs, especially in Africa, if we ran more of our own development projects; and, within developing countries, from those who think local NGOs have failed and that large international agencies can 'do' development better. Conspiracy theorists may detect a political thrust here, which those who believe in empowering development will wish to resist.

This is not to say that there is any significant trend among donors towards managing their own projects, although this may come in the future. The heavy management and resource costs of operational development work are a potent deterrent. The point is that today donors are expecting to exert more influence over the management of the projects which they fund, and that this is altering the older donor/partner relationship.

Partner-centred development philosophy: the case of Oxfam

The Northern context has also radically changed, as can be seen in the case of Oxfam. In the 1970s and 1980s, Oxfam developed its priorities and work styles largely with reference to partners. In the mid-1980s, the field offices were even asked to debate formal mechanisms for incorporating a 'partner voice'. Several country and regional offices set up consultative committees of 'friends of Oxfam', or regular meetings of partners. These structures were mostly advisory, and it was only in India that the process went to the point where devolution of power — what Oxfam calls 'transfer of Trustee responsibility' — was considered in detail.

Beyond the debates about the mechanisms for involving partners, there was an almost universal commitment to putting their interests first. The country and regional office teams which rejected formal consultation with partners — as did the Latin America and Caribbean offices — passionately believed in sharing with partners and argued that what mattered more than formalities was the commitment of the Representative and her/his team. All agreed on the fundamental point: 'engagement' with the social issues of the time and sympathy with the development philosophy of counterparts was the key. It became a major factor in Oxfam's recruitment of programme staff. Country policies were strongly influenced by certain key national NGOs whose work pushed back the frontiers of development analysis and practice, often taking great risks in the process. In the Oxford headquarters, the Desks, the Overseas Directorate, and the specialist Trustee Committees shared and supported this philosophical framework. Elsewhere in Oxfam the growth of campaigning in the UK — which was developed by a former Representative in Brazil — was very much designed to provide Northern support for Southern partners. In short, Oxfam took its development agenda from its partners. Where this agenda had to be negotiated to accommodate the constraints and needs which Oxfam faced in the UK context, in compliance with charity law and to meet the requirements of fund-raising from a British public generally ignorant of partner philosophies, the practice was to defend the overseas programme to the last gasp.

Today the picture is different and more complicated. Far more important than before are Oxfam's institutional interests in fund-raising, in maintaining a high media profile in the eyes of the British public relative to other agencies, and in acquiring influence with national and international political elites. These interests are no longer secondary to programme work as previously defined; instead they are co-equal priorities to be placed uneasily alongside the mandates which come from partners and beneficiaries in the South. The primacy of 'the overseas programme' is being replaced by a search for a nebulous 'one programme', in which older and newer interests have to be reconciled. The debate in Oxfam today concerns how this reconciliation is to take place, and who is to decide its terms. This rapidly becomes a philosophical debate about development values, and the accountability and mandate of Oxfam, which is beyond the scope of this article. One might only observe that it may be a measure of the wider crisis in development thinking and practice referred to above that Oxfam — and it is not alone in this — has yet to address these issues adequately, despite a recent large-scale strategic planning exercise within the Overseas Division.

What value do we donors add?

A question not often addressed in debates about the donor/partner/beneficiary relationship is what value the first adds, apart from granting funds? What can Oxfam and the others do better than our partners? The challenge should make us think before we make rash claims about donors being 'good at' (for example) low-level community work. What an agency like Oxfam can add to the relationship probably includes:

• *Untied funds which can be applied flexibly and rapidly*. Few financial institutions in the public and private sectors, however large they are, have as much scope with the use of their budgets. Government and bilateral donors approve and pay grants extremely slowly, compared with many NGOs. Donor NGO grant budgets are perhaps not always used as effectively as possible. Possibly donors err on the side of renewing grants to the same projects year after year, rather than constantly and imaginatively reviewing the best use of their funds. Greater priority currently attached by many donors to planning and continuity — rather than

to strategic thinking and change — may further discourage flexibility and quick response.

• *Traditions of disinterested, non-aligned, bottom-up development*. Not many donors come with as little ideological baggage as Oxfam carries. This gives scope for support of groups which others might shy away from, as well as credibility with decision takers and opinion formers.

• *Risk-taking*. This may be a surprising assertion, but the fact is that partners battling away on the front lines of development have much less scope to take risks than does a prestigious international institution like Oxfam. Are we being as bold as we can and should be, in development work in the South as well as in advocacy in the North? How do we evaluate this?

• *World-wide experience and contacts*. The potential for supporting partners by providing information and exchange opportunities in the overseas programmes of the larger donors is considerable. This learning from experience (called in Oxfam 'institutional learning') and networking potential is almost completely unrealised in Oxfam, and probably to varying extents in most of the other major donors. The problem is recognised, but, despite efforts, little progress has been made in finding solutions.

• *Advocacy and communication*. More and more donors accept a responsibility to use their individual and collective influence to support partners with contributions to public-policy debate, speaking on their behalf and arguing for changes in international (and sometimes intra-national) relationships. This is an area where significant 'donor value' may be added. At the same time, there must be questions about where the agenda of current lobbying comes from, and how it fits with programme work. This is controversial. One view is that lobbying or advocacy is an important and logical extension of the prescriptions of the micro-projects supported in development programmes. Another is that Northern lobbying has become disconnected from specific Southern political and development positions and is now governed by a generalists', Northern-based development agenda.

There are other stake-holders in this debate. Among these are the fund-raisers and their interest in raising the agency's public profile. There is a *quid pro quo* offered between lobbyist and fund-raiser: the former raises the profile of the organisation, while the latter uses the high profile to raise the funds. This is a new alliance being formed in the Northern donor world, and it will be important to evaluate the reaction of the other groups interested in the lobbying agenda, particularly the development programme staff (on the one hand) and (on the other) the emergency departments (who have traditionally been the agency profile-raisers). Donors are wrestling with the problem of shifting alliances and competition between development, emergency, fund-raising, and public relations/advocacy interests. The danger is that, in this internal debate, the views of partners and beneficiaries are not given enough prominence.

Conclusion

In the 1990s, Northern development NGO donors are moving away from some of the assumptions of development practice in the last two decades. This has led to questioning of relationships with Southern NGOs and to re-examination of the comparative advantages and distinctive contributions of different donors. However, in this necessary process of review, the challenge is to carry through our mandate, which remains to seek change which will eliminate poverty and poverty-related injustice. We need to criticise generalisations and out-moded assumptions, and develop criteria which will help us and our partners to be more effective in the common cause. We must thus guard against pressures in the North which would divert us from our central, historical mission which lines us up shoulder to shoulder with the poor in their (and dare one still say our?) struggle against injustice and poverty.

Notes

1 An earlier version of this paper was written as a contribution to the strategic planning debate within Oxfam (UK and Ireland). All references to Oxfam are to Oxfam UK and Ireland. The views expressed are the author's own and are not necessarily those of Oxfam UK/I.

2 It must be emphasised that this discussion concerns development work, not short-term emergency relief. The points that will be made about empowerment and accountability to the beneficiaries may not be as directly relevant (although they will be indirectly relevant) where the issue is the provision of rapidly delivered aid to save lives.

The author

Richard Moseley-Williams is the Regional Coordinator for Latin America and the Caribbean at ACTIONAID. Previously, he worked at Oxfam (UK/I) for 15 years as Coordinator of the Latin America and Caribbean programme and, from 1991 to 1993, as Regional Manager for South Africa, Zimbabwe, and Namibia. This article first appeared in *Development in Practice* Volume 4, Number 1, in 1994.

NGOs and social change:
agents or facilitators?

Jenny Pearce

Introduction

The opportunity for NGOs to move from 'a *doing* to an *influencing* role' (to quote from John Clark's recent book *Democratising Development*[1]) originates partly from the 'push' of voluntary agencies themselves, many of which have proved more effective in poverty alleviation and development than their official counterparts. And partly it originates from the 'pull' of the 'official' development world, which has begun to recognise the competence of NGOs and offer them real space and resources. This has led many to see ever-increasing potential in NGOs as *agents*, rather than *facilitators* of development. The need to 'scale up' has been identified as a way for NGOs to move from a purely local impact to national influence via networking, coordinating, advocacy, and developing a strategic way of thinking.

Many of these issues arise from recent articles in *Development in Practice* by Michael Edwards and David Hulme[2] and John Clark[3] himself. I wish here to concentrate on:

- *The definition of NGOs*: are grassroots or popular organisations usefully put into the same category as intermediary institutions?

- *The appropriate role of NGOs*: can we universally assume that by virtue of being outside the State, NGOs represent a force for democratising development?

- *The relationship of NGOs and the community, and NGOs and the State*: is the emphasis on the need to 'scale up' and seek wider influence premature, where NGOs have not worked out their relationship with their local constituencies and 'beneficiaries'?

What are NGOs?

Many definitions encompass such a range of organisations that 'NGO' ceases to be a useful category with which to work. John Clark is not alone in using 'NGO' as a catch-all term for a variety of different non-State organisations. Definitions usually range from *popular organisations* to *intermediary development organisations*, whether indigenous or externally-funded, specialist or general, and *international organisations*, such as Oxfam. It is the inclusion of grassroots or popular organisations within this general category which troubles me and which is partly responsible for the shift in perception of the role of NGOs from facilitators to agents of change. Among the fundamental differences between popular organisations and NGOs, I would emphasise the following:

1 *Social composition*: Popular organisations consist of people with specific identities and interests, dependent on their class, gender, ethnic origin, or cultural background, who have come together out of their own need for collective representation and organisation. Intermediary NGOs are typically composed of middle-class people who have opted, for political or humanitarian reasons, to work with (or on behalf of) the poor and marginalised.

2 *Organisations versus institutions*: Popular organisations are not institutions, but dynamic organisations which represent specific social interests. They may be externally funded, though the impact of this has often been divisive and corrupting. Thus many international NGOs prefer to use — and often themselves create — intermediary bodies to work with popular organisations. Such bodies are institutions, with relatively formal, permanent structures which aim to survive not on the basis of the interests of a particular social constituency, but on that of their perceived efficiency and effectiveness, at least in the eyes of their external funders.

3 *The significance of intermediary NGOs*: Intermediary NGOs (John Clark's category of 'popular development agencies'), although they exist to facilitate links between 'beneficiaries' on the one hand and their funders on the other, are often, and paradoxically, accountable to their funders in a way they are not to their 'beneficiaries'. The latter do not elect members of NGOs to represent them, and rarely have the chance to choose between one NGO and another. Nor do funding agencies, in my experience, consult with 'beneficiaries' when decisions are made to fund intermediary NGOs. It is all too easy, therefore, for local development NGOs to carry the agendas of Northern funders to their work, rather than represent the interests of the people they support. I am certainly not implying that popular organisations are necessarily accountable or internally democratic. But their problems of accountability derive from factors of a social and political, rather than economic, nature.

It is not helpful to use the term 'NGO' to encompass popular organisations as well as those intermediary institutions established to provide care, facilitate self-help and grass-roots democracy, to supply technical assistance, or to campaign on issues of importance to the poor.

The failure to make these distinctions contributes to a tendency to depoliticise popular organisations and politicise development NGOs.

In practice, of course, the World Bank and other international agencies *do* acknowledge the distinction. When recognising the role of NGOs, they are not envisaging peasants organising to defend their land rights or workers organising for better pay and conditions. They have in mind the voluntary organisations who may be able to deliver services more efficiently than the State. They equate NGOs with a regenerated private sector; their importance lies in simply being outside the State, which is held to be responsible for the development failings of the last two decades.[4]

What is the appropriate role of NGOs?

A great many claims are currently being made about NGOs, based on their supposed capacity to do the following:

- 'Democratise development.'
- Reconstruct or construct 'civil society'.
- Act as social mobilisers.
- Deliver services more efficiently than the State.
- Be more flexible, and show greater capacity for innovations and closer identification with the targeted sectors of aid.
- Contribute to strengthening the development model offered by the private sector.

NGOs are seen as having such potential partly because of the global shift in political and economic theories. Politically, there is the collapse of the reforming and revolutionary-left project, with its emphasis on State power. Economically, there is the rise of neo-liberal economics, and its emphasis on the retreat of the State and development led by the private sector.

Within this context, NGOs have become something which everybody can love, but which mean very different things to everyone. The World Bank can see them as efficient non-State channels in an era of anti-Statism. Progressive international donors, on the other hand, can see them as a means of helping the poor and powerless. In focusing on NGOs as if they had a common role and common characteristics, we may conceal the failure of many to measure up to the ideal, and the dangers of 'scaling up' when accountability to their beneficiaries is so ambiguous.

NGOs, empowerment, and civil society

The crucial question here is: *in what circumstances, and how, do intermediary development NGOs play a role in enhancing the ability of the poor both to meet their material needs and to ensure that they have an impact on the structures of power around them?* In other words, how can we establish criteria for evaluating the impact of their work? And how do we return to seeing NGOs as *facilitators* of development processes, at the grassroots, rather than as *agents* of change?

A facilitating role is central to the notion of 'empowerment', which is surely about passing power on to those who have none, not about building up the power of those assisting in the process itself. However, there is a growing tension in some parts of Latin America — particularly Central America and Chile, where a great deal of external funding was channelled through NGOs during politically sensitive periods — between the increasing institutional capacity and resources of the intermediary NGOs, and the under-resourced popular organisations which they were set up to assist. The uneasy relationship between the two entails a real possibility of rifts and disillusionment.

Undeniably, political change is taking place which will open up spaces for previously excluded organisations in many Southern societies. Understandably, in countries where there has been a history of repressive, interventionist States, people look positively on the emergence of non-government organisations within society. The increasing interest in the concept of 'civil society' has itself contributed to the view that the NGOs can both strengthen and help to construct a sphere which will protect society from a return to the intrusive State.

The term 'civil society' crops up increasingly in contemporary development literature, particularly on Africa. However, unless we become more rigorous, the term may mask, rather than illuminate, a dynamic in the South which is just as likely to produce greater inequalities, political polarisation, and social exclusion as it is to be a democratising force. For example, it is true that, during the 1980s, popular mobilisations were important in the transition from military to civilian rule in some parts of Latin America; or have forced elections in some African countries and challenged the one-party State. Clark writes:

In much of Latin America throughout the eighties the failure of left-wing political parties to win power, resist repression or reflect the day-to-day concerns of the majority of the poor created a political space for popular movements. Throughout the region ordinary people saw their battles being fought not by opposition parties but by popular movements ... While initially reactive — responding to situations created by others — the popular movements have gone on to create the political agenda.[5]

However, the point about these 'social movements' was their spontaneous nature. Intermediary NGOs may occasionally have played a supporting role. But they were not responsible for the social mobilisation itself.

'Social movements' are characterised by their lack of permanence and their fragility: they are often an eruption of protest, rather than the result of sustained organisational work. More significantly, in Latin America they have widely failed to survive the very transitions from authoritarian rule to which they contributed. Chile is the classic case, but not the only one. Here, the return to civilian rule — which was eventually negotiated by political elites — has been accompanied by the disempowerment of the social movements of the 1980s. The Chilean NGO world is split between those who opted to engage with the centre-left government programme — and so have succeeded in institutionalising themselves in the new circumstances — and those who remain critical of the failure of the government to meet the needs of the poorest sectors. The latter remain small, under-resourced, fragmented, and politically marginalised. And, as the larger NGOs have come closer to the national and formal 'political' world, their links with the social world have become very weak.

The case of Chile illustrates that the 'social movements' of the 1980s emphasised the *weakness* of 'civil society', not its arrival on the scene. People had taken to the streets, precisely because the appropriate channels for political participation did not exist for them.

The role of NGOs in 'civil society'

There are two strands to the concept of 'civil society'. One lies within the European liberal political theory and the challenge to the absolutist State in the seventeenth and eighteenth centuries. As Western Europe industrialised, so the concepts of the 'private' and the 'public' spheres began to emerge. The former was that of male property holders who asserted the rights of the individual to operate freely in the market place, without the intrusion of the State. Sovereignty was to lie with these individuals, who consented to the existence of the State, as long as it limited its role to areas defined by these individuals. Civil society, or 'civil government' in John Locke's terminology, referred to the development of a sphere outside the State.

For many Western governments and official aid agencies today, the retreat of the State as the agent of development gives rise to the need for a 'private' sphere, both to ensure that the State is accountable within a limited role, and to encourage the private entrepreneur as a motor for development. Thus, the resurgence of the concept of 'civil society' reflects the resurgence of the neoliberal economic paradigm.

By contrast, Marxist thinking emphasises the inequality within civil society, since the State is seen to be a reflection of the rule of one class over another. That the State can be a totalitarian and repressive force is now widely recognised across the political spectrum.

The poor as well as the rich want to ensure that the State is representative and accountable. But to abandon the analysis of inequalities within 'civil society', simply because we recognise the role for an appropriate sphere of life outside the State, does not follow.

Some writers do acknowledge the need to be more precise in defining 'civil society'. Hugh Roberts, for example, argues that the discussion should focus on enfranchisement and citizenship:

... 'civil society' exists where society enjoys a **particular** *kind of regular (not occasional) relationship to the State, founded upon the fact of enfranchisement in its substantive rather than merely formal sense and thus upon the existence of the effective status of citizens which its members possess with all the rights* vis à vis *the State which this status entails.*[6]

This raises many issues with respect to popular organisations and intermediary development NGOs. In most of Latin America, for example, the basic rights of citizenship exist in formal rather than substantive terms. The impunity of those responsible for the violations of human rights over the last decade demonstrates that even the rule of law does not apply to the powerful. An authentic civil society must involve the poor and the weak gaining real and meaningful rights as citizens, genuinely enfranchised and able to build organisations to defend their interests. It is about the rights of individuals to associate voluntarily. Constructing civil society cannot be essentially about building up intermediary development organisations to represent the 'poor': it must be about empowering the poor and enabling them to fight for their own rights as citizens.

In many parts of the South, not only are there vast inequalities in social and economic resources and power, and often dubious commitment to real political enfranchisement (electoral fraud is rife in many countries), but there is no commitment to the idea of the *social rights of citizenship*. Where the poor come together, they are certainly concerned with their political rights. But they are often anxious to ensure that the State grants, and then protects, social rights. However, the prevailing pattern is for the State to retreat. Structural adjustment programmes have in many cases decimated State benefits to the poor, such as food subsidies, which had previously existed. Neo-liberal policies will undoubtedly exacerbate existing inequalities, even if (and this remains to be proved) they bring about sustainable economic growth.

Strengthening the ability of poor women and men in the South to fight for their full citizenship rights is a priority, but will also generate conflict. In Western Europe, for at least 200 years, 'civil society' consisted only of male property-holders. Conflicts emerged when the poor, and women, demanded political enfranchisement and social rights. The same sectors of the South will make similar demands — and indeed they will have to, if they are to enjoy the fruits of development.[7]

Intermediary development NGOs can act as catalysts in helping and supporting poor and marginalised people. However, they cannot substitute for the poor themselves. Without meaningful accountability to their 'beneficiaries', scaling them up could seriously distance them from the poor and their own social structures.

NGOs and the community, and NGOs and the State

The real challenge in development is less about how to influence national events and international policy (though this is evidently important too), and more about building *sustainable social processes* from below, to ensure genuine empowerment at the grassroots. The objective of development 'from below' is surely that the poor and powerless identify their own needs and interests, and gain a means to shape policies affecting them. This does not mean that intermediary development NGOs do not have their own role to play, or that people who work within them do not have their own interests to fight for. It does mean that if they aim genuinely to contribute to the process of social change at the grassroots, there must be evidence that the men and women they work with are increasingly able to effect changes in their own lives, by their own efforts.

In my 20 years' experience in Latin America, such empowerment is by no means a given. Precisely because many NGOs emerged at a time when structural political change was on the agenda, many focused on how they could bring it

about, at the expense of processes in which they were involved. The high degree of gender-blindness, the hierarchical nature of decision-making within many NGOs, and the tendency to institutionalise themselves rather than building up the capacity of the poor to run their own affairs all point to the widespread neglect of the *processes* of change at the grassroots.

This is not to say that political change has ceased to be important. It is as important as ever. My purpose is to draw attention to the fact that now, above all, we should give greater emphasis to understanding the social processes which are so important to generating meaningful and sustainable changes in people's lives. The most technical and assistential of development programmes has an impact on the social relations of the group concerned. But many NGOs seem more concerned with an influencing role *vis à vis* the State, or with enhancing their technical capacity and efficiency, than with examining their own relationship and impact on the communities with which they work.

Social processes are messy and difficult to measure. An important task facing us now is to identify criteria to determine why we support some NGOs rather than others. Academics and practitioners could work together in drawing on the long field experience of intermediary development organisations and analysing what underlies the success or failure of particular programmes. This will help to avoid the trap of 'NGO' becoming the latest development buzzword, attracting funds to strengthen the institutional capacity of these organisations, with no guarantee of their effectiveness at the social level.

Notes

1 John Clark: *Democratising Development: The Role of Voluntary Organisations*, London: Earthscan, 1991.
2 Michael Edwards and David Hulme: 'Scaling up NGO impact on development: learning from experience', *Development in Practice*, Vol. 2, No. 2: 77–91, 1992.
3 John Clark: 'Democratising development: NGOs and the State', *Development in Practice*, Vol. 2, No. 3: 151–62, 1992.

4 Hugh Roberts, in an Editorial in the *IDS Bulletin*, Vol. 18, No. 41 (1987), argues that while the emergence of new private-sector groups as the State retreats may be the only way of sustaining a more balanced and equitable development in tropical Africa, it might also merely allow new elite farmer groups to emerge, able to extract regionally, ethnically, and socially specific concessions from the State to the detriment of other classes and groups with less muscle. It is therefore necessary to distinguish a State which is weak in relation to an increasingly developed civil society of self-sustaining voluntary associations which can make it accountable to them, and a State which is weak because it is open to the influences of traditional patron–client networks and ethnic solidarities. A State could also be weak *vis à vis* a vibrant civil society, but more able to fulfil its functions to look after the general interest, and more capable in that sense.

5 John Clark, 1991, op. cit.

6 Hugh Roberts, 1987, op. cit., p. 4.

7 This is where we come to the essential problems of the democracy debate in the South. The problem of representative democracy as it has emerged in the advanced capitalist countries is that it combines equality of political rights with considerable social and economic inequality.

T. H. Marshall's classic study of citizenship (*Citizenship and Social Class and Other Essays*, Cambridge: Cambridge University Press, 1950) examines the relationship between citizenship and social class in Britain. He identifies three stages in the development of citizenship rights: the civil element was about individual rights and emerged with the rise of the market economy; the political part of citizenship concerns the right to participate in the exercise of political power; and the social element of citizenship is the right to the prevailing standard of living. Marshall believed that the Welfare State had been able to alleviate the worst aspects of the social inequalities which remain in democratic capitalist societies.

The author

Jenny Pearce is currently a Lecturer in the Department of Peace Studies at the University of Bradford. Previously she was Director of Latin America Bureau, and is the author of several books on development and politics in the region. For many years she has been closely connected with major UK NGOs, including Oxfam and Christian Aid. This article was first published in *Development in Practice* Volume 3, Number 3, in 1993.

On being evaluated: tensions and hopes

Movimento de Organização Comunitária

The Movimento de Organização Comunitária (MOC) (Movement for Community Organisation) is a multi-disciplinary advisory centre for community organisations in the Feira de Santana region of north-east Brazil. It has worked for over 25 years in educational and social organisation, in areas including agriculture, appropriate technology, health care, women's organisation, small-scale economic projects, trades unions, and cultural expression.

Oxfam (UK and Ireland) began funding MOC's work in 1972, and by 1988 was meeting approximately 7 per cent of its total budget. In 1990/91 Oxfam commissioned a Brazilian institution — the Joaquim Nabuco Foundation — to conduct an evaluation, comprising extensive interviews with MOC staff and a limited amount of field-based research in the communities within which MOC was operating.

Oxfam continued to fund MOC's work after the conclusion of the evaluation, but, following shifts in its own funding priorities, does not plan further support beyond its current commitment.

This article (translated by the Editor from Portuguese) was written by MOC to convey what it felt like to be the object of an evaluation.

The evaluation proposal

NGOs, including MOC, usually include evaluation in their on-going activities. Often, however, donor agencies insist on evaluations with very specific and detailed objectives, to involve or be co-ordinated by outsiders. This was what Oxfam proposed. How did we feel about it?

The first question was whether we could realistically say 'No' to the proposal. After all, we were dealing with our funders. In the end, we felt we could not very well refuse. At least, it would not have been polite to do so.

Another issue worried us: who would carry out the evaluation? What would their connections be? What ideological positions would they represent? And who would see the final report? MOC has links with many local organisations and funding agencies. Each donor agency tends to earmark its support for a defined area of our work, and so has very specific expectations of us. The possible repercussions arising from the evaluation were a real worry for us. This has a lot to do with how the funding agencies behave and pool information among themselves. For example, some were asking us to share the report with them, even before the information-gathering phase had been completed.

Another issue was that, since we were being evaluated, our own competence was implicitly on the line. To an extent, the survival of the organisation was in the balance. But who is to say what competence means in the context of social organisation? Oxfam always claimed that the evaluation had nothing to do with whether funding would continue or not. Our own feeling, however, was that any new grants would depend on a positive outcome from the evaluation.

All this meant that we had mixed feelings about the evaluation. On the one hand, outsiders were invading our space, questioning things to which we were committed and which meant a lot to us — and so passing judgement on our lives. On the other hand, it was an opportunity to question ourselves, to look more deeply at our work, without getting too emotionally involved. Also, since we were experiencing some internal conflict over what we were doing and why, the evaluation offered the chance to express these concerns, and might give us some insights into how we could improve our contribution to the popular movement.

The evaluation process

The way the evaluation process developed was enriching as well as contradictory. In a sense, it forced us to sit down, reflect, and learn from what we were doing.

One particularly positive aspect of the experience was the one-to-one interviews which the researchers held with each member of the team, which helped us to reflect on the work and not just reply off the top of our heads. There were also some collective sessions, which were quite revealing.

They asked us for a lot of information: about the life of the organisation, how it related to the broader social context and so on, and about the detail of our projects, accounts, procedures, and reports. This called for an enormous effort on our part, but we tried to engage in the process confidently and openly, precisely because we were the ones with something at stake. Everything we said and did was checked. From time to time, however, we began to wonder: were we being serious, straightforward, or just naive? Was it worth being so open and sincere?

Because of what it represented, the evaluation was in fact a burden, whatever the good intentions of the evaluators. Not everyone felt like going along with it. Sometimes we got the feeling that we were under surveillance. In the field visits, when the evaluators were accompanied by team members, we were sometimes tempted just to show them the aspects of our work which we knew were functioning well. In fact, we deliberately selected groups for the case study which we knew were undergoing major problems; we raised questions which would reveal personal connections in some projects; we questioned authoritarian behaviour among community leaders, and so on. In the end, we opted for being totally open in sharing documentation and information about MOC.

For us, the whole business was marred by a mixture of tensions: the need to keep faith with the process (after all, the renewal of the funding agreement depended on the outcome!); an inconclusive discussion about our objectives; and finally, the personal evaluation of everyone involved. Yet, at the same time, we were very hopeful that the process would give us the basis on which to confirm our own direction.

The report and discussion

After the information-gathering phase and subsequent discussions in the communities, we received the first draft of the evaluation report. It was a valuable document about the MOC — our objectives, engagement, and philosophy — and case studies of some of the communities. However, partly because of its scope and the short time it took to complete the research, partly because of the limitations of the research team, the report had little impact on MOC's work: it certainly did not meet our expectations.

In the first place, the issues which it raised, as far as we were concerned, needed to be explored more fully. Secondly, in spite of our hopes, it gave us few useful insights. Thirdly, we found certain conclusions about the MOC, and some of our partner groups, rather distorted.

There was one meeting between the researchers and the MOC team, together with Oxfam, to discuss the final report, in which we put forward all our points of disagreement with it. However, the atmosphere did not make for an open discussion. On the contrary, it seemed to us that everyone came to the table with their prejudices intact, so that the meeting contributed little to the process as a whole. Few modifications of substance were introduced into the report.

We felt frustrated about all the things which were not raised in the final document. We felt threatened by the impact that it might have on others, including the funding agencies, especially given its failure to convey accurately who we are and what we aim to do. We feel that we became the *objects* of an evaluation which misrepresented our work — and that of the communities — without allowing us the right to defend ourselves. Essentially, we felt that we had become the object of decisions which were to be taken bilaterally by the Foundation and Oxfam. We thus decided to suspend the final part of the process: a seminar with various Bahian organisations about the results.

While we had seen the evaluation as a process and not as a document, what predominated was the fixation on the report. Since the report in question was one with which we could not agree, the gap between ourselves and the evaluators grew wider. Eventually, we decided to hold a slightly different seminar, just for representatives of the organisations involved in the evaluation, run by a facilitator. While it was heavy-going to begin with, this managed to clear the air a bit, making it possible for people to discuss the process, the methodology, and fieldwork, more calmly. Everyone acknowledged their faults and their strengths. It was a step forward. We had acted sincerely, and reached some rich and profound conclusions.

Some conclusions

We believe that there are some useful lessons to come out of this process, which can help everyone involved in evaluations.

1 An evaluation proposal must be discussed fully and clearly, allowing everyone to explain their particular way of seeing things, express their expectations, and explore their concerns, in order to reduce the scope for misunderstandings.

2 We Southern NGOs must develop the capacity to reflect on our work and be clear about when and under what conditions we think evaluations should take place. In this way, we can be straightforward and open with Northern donor agencies in deciding, on a more objective basis, whether it is appropriate to embark on any particular evaluation process. In our opinion, we are rarely free to do this. And what would the Northern NGOs think of the idea? What is certain is that we get involved in one evaluation after another, without any of them really helping us to be more effective in achieving our aims.

3 It is imperative to ensure a proper match between the nature of the work to be evaluated and the expertise of the evaluators, especially in the area of social organisation with popular sectors. Only then will an appropriate methodology be agreed.

4 In our view, it is crucial that evaluation should be a collective process, not one in which we are treated or made to feel as though we are just an object. The main thing is that evaluation should help us to think more deeply about what we are doing, drawing the lessons and redirecting our work, if necessary. We have no wish to be objects of studies and research.

5 Donor agencies and local organisations need to learn how to deal with the question of evaluation more calmly, more self-critically, and more honestly. Of course, evaluation is absolutely fundamental: it has to happen and should never be ignored. But decisions cannot be made unilaterally, because so much depends on timing, practicalities, the choice of evaluators, and so on. Everyone involved needs to understand the objectives and agree with the choice of evaluation methods. For the most part, academic research methodologies are inappropriate for evaluating social organisation work.

There are many other issues we could raise, but the above comments are enough to give an idea of our concerns, our feelings, our ideas, and the way in which we have developed, as a group, in the process. Now, of course, we are more experienced; and we hope to have contributed to setting the framework for better and clearer relationships between local organisations and donor agencies, in the context of evaluation.

(This article first appeared in *Development in Practice,* Volume 3, Number 3, in 1993.)

Sustainability is not about money!: the case of the Belize Chamber of Commerce and Industry

Deryck R Brown

Recent concern over the sustainability of development institutions almost invariably seems to focus on the financial aspects of the problem. Donors provide project funding within a specified time frame and expect that, when the funding comes to an end, recipient institutions will have mapped out a strategy for cost-recovery or meeting recurrent expenditure that will enable them to continue producing goods/services well into the future. This article, which is informed by insights gleaned during the course of a study of institutional sustainability in Central America and the Caribbean (Brown 1996), takes the view that the tendency to equate sustainability with financial self-sufficiency and to concentrate efforts on revenue generation is in fact a mistake and a potentially disastrous distraction for an institution implementing a development programme. Sustainability and development objectives conflict, and the institution is pulled in different directions. Since the pressures for sustainability are often more intense (and more difficult to resist) than the developmental goals, the institution can easily lose sight of the latter as sustainability itself becomes the main goal.

To illustrate the point, let us consider the case of the Belize Chamber of Commerce and Industry (BCCI), which was the executing agency for a USAID-funded project worth some US$2.5 million between 1986 and 1993. The purpose of the project was 'to develop the capacity of the private sector to promote, provide technical assistance for and facilitate export and tourism-related projects as well as to facilitate (foreign) investments in Belize' (BCCI 1994). The BCCI presents a stark example of an institution where, under pressure from and with the full support and encouragement of the donor, sustainability was perceived in purely financial terms and became an end in itself, instead of a means to an end. The case is offered here not as a typical example, but merely as evidence of what can go wrong in such circumstances.

Sustainability and the recurrent-cost problem

Studies of institutional sustainability always return to one basic theme: meeting recurrent costs. Even those studies which begin by explicitly eschewing the financial interpretation of the problem (such as Brinkerhoff and Goldsmith 1990; Brinkerhoff 1992a, 1992b; Finsterbusch 1990; Gustafson 1994; LaFond 1995; SIDA 1995) seem to end up exactly where they claim not to be starting off.

There is no gainsaying the importance of financial viability in continuing activities begun with donor assistance. There is compelling evidence that, where the government or some other agent in the recipient country fails to step in to fill the vacuum left by the donor's withdrawal, the project-initiated activity suffers a loss of quality or ceases altogether (SIDA 1991; LaFond 1995). *Ex post* evaluations of numerous projects have found low levels of sustainability several years after project completion. In many cases, quality tends to be high while external funding is available to pay for staff, overheads, equipment, and consumables. Once the funds run out, however, it is often impossible to maintain those levels of production, because local funders are either unwilling or unable to provide funds at the same level as external donors.

Because the donor's most obvious contribution is financial, finding alternative sources of funds becomes a major preoccupation for recipient institutions as the project-completion date approaches. This drive for financial self-sufficiency is not merely encouraged but actually demanded by donor agencies. Recipients therefore devote considerable time and resources to identifying ways of generating income that could be applied to the recurrent expenditure of the programme.

Generally speaking, two strategies can be employed for revenue-generation. First, the recipient might introduce cost-recovery charges and user-fees in an attempt, at the very least, to make the programme's output pay for itself. Secondly, the recipient might consider diversifying its activities and moving into areas which it perceives as being profitable. These two options are by no means mutually exclusive; each one is accompanied by its own set of considerations, trade-offs, and pitfalls.

On the down side, introducing cost-recovery charges and user-fees can lead to a form of price discrimination which serves to exclude the intended beneficiaries and threatens the developmental objective of reaching the very poorest. To address this concern, two variants of this option might emerge. First, prices are set at a level that ensures equity but at the same time generates minimal income, thereby rendering as farce any idea of financial self-sufficiency. The second possibility is the introduction of a 'two-tiered' system, in which one set of 'fee-based' goods or services is offered to the lower-income clients.

Product-diversification, on the other hand, involves the identification and introduction of a new activity as an ancillary or adjunct to the programme's main, 'proper' core activity. The idea is that the new activity will be the money-spinner and will be approached from the outset as a 'business' intended to yield a profit which can be ploughed back into the main programme. Small-scale credit is an especially popular activity from this standpoint, as it is widely perceived that credit is one of the few activities with an intrinsic revenue-generating capacity. There is little doubt that this is a major reason why NGOs, in particular, gravitate towards microfinance (cf Dichter 1995; Hulme and Mosley 1996). But credit is not the only ancillary activity contemplated; these can range from renting out property and offering blood-testing facilities to the provision of professional consultancy services and, as we shall see in the case of the BCCI, the establishment of a lottery (lotto) game (Brown 1996).

Background to the BCCI project

The Belize Chamber of Commerce and Industry is a membership organisation, set up since 1920 as the representative body of big commercial enterprises in Belize City. It has grown into a national businesspeople's association which represents the interests of the private sector to government and foreign investors. From 1986, through its technical arm, BEIPU (Belize Export and Investment Promotion Unit), it got involved in the areas of investment-promotion and export-development, particularly the promotion of non-traditional exports.

Until 1986, the BCCI's only source of income was contributions/subscriptions from members, which never exceeded Bz$100,000 (Bz$1= US$0.50) annually. In 1986, however, the Chamber signed a Cooperative Agreement with USAID by which approximately Bz$5.7 million was provided by the latter over a seven-year period (1986–1993). These funds were to be used to develop the private sector's capacity, particularly in the fields of non-traditional exports and tourism.

Between 1989 and 1993, the BCCI grew into a national development agency with chapters (or divisions) in each district of Belize. Membership grew from under 100 to 622, of which 80 per cent were small and micro enterprises. The activities of the Chamber came to embrace both economic and social development through employment-creation, attracting foreign direct investment, export-development, and the provision of business information. During the project period it conducted over 30 workshops; delivered training and provided direct assistance to small entrepreneurs; organised missions to more than 30 international trade fairs; produced various publications and marketing materials, including an investment brochure and video as well as a monthly newsletter for the business community; provided guidance and assistance to farmers and manufacturers in exporting their products; and participated in the establishment of a Junior Achievement Programme in 17 high schools.

The Chamber also set up a Policy and Planning Unit to deal, among other things, with a number of trade issues and to facilitate inward investment; provided a full range of consultancy services using Belizean consultants; and funded a pilot credit scheme through the National Development Foundation of Belize (also a USAID-funded institution). It served as a catalyst for expanded economic activities in Belize and contributed significantly to the development of a viable handicraft industry in the country. Audited financial statements of the BCCI showed that annual expenditure averaged Bz$1.5 million, of which 50 per cent was spent though BEIPU on developmental projects and a further 10 per cent was spent on the development of the handicraft industry (BCCI 1994).

From all indications, the programme was reasonably successful, and a USAID evaluation gave the Chamber high marks for its pivotal role in promoting and facilitating economic expansion and job-creation, as well as regional integration. In particular, the Chamber was commended for stimulating and improving the local handicraft industry (closely allied to tourism) and the non-traditional export sector (USAID 1992).

Recognising that funding from USAID was coming to an end, and under pressure from the donor to demonstrate its potential sustainability as reflected in revenue generated, the BCCI's

Executive Council and management began to consider alternative sources of income which would enable it to continue delivering its developmental services beyond the end of the project. One overriding consideration was that the Chamber could not enter into activities which competed with its members. The Chamber therefore devised and agreed upon a three-pronged strategy for achieving sustainability in 1992, as follows:

- expanding and retaining its membership;
- becoming the local agent for Western Union in the money-transfer business;
- establishing a national lottery (Lotto) game to be administered for a fee.

Essentially, the plan was that revenues from the Lotto game would replace USAID's funding, thereby allowing the BCCI to continue its developmental activities. But the initial enthusiasm for the game, combined with other circumstances, led the Chamber to lose sight of its mission. It became so preoccupied with its new 'money-spinner' and the idea of becoming sustainable in the narrow financial sense that its developmental activities were neglected. Thus the programme for which sustainability was sought in the first place was supplanted by an activity which could succeed in solving the recurrent-cost problem, but delivered no developmental benefits whatsoever.

The Lotto game

The BCCI entered into an understanding with the Government of Belize (GoB) in 1992 to establish the Lotto game, whereby the GoB would own 60 per cent of the enterprise and the Chamber the remaining 40 per cent. A sudden change of government, however, prompted a new agreement by which the GoB held 100 per cent ownership of the game and the BCCI was contracted to manage it for a period of five years. Technical support and other assistance with the setting up of the Lotto game, including the procurement of equipment, was provided by a Canadian financial group, CBN. Estimates prepared by CBN suggested that sales in the first

12 months would amount to at least Bz$14 million (BCCI 1994).

The game was eventually launched in December 1993, but in its first 11 months ticket sales fell far short of the estimate. In fact, total sales were less than Bz$2 million. Because of the disappointing performance, the BCCI was unable to meet its contractual obligations to both the GoB and CBN, as their shares of the proceeds were diverted to meeting the costs involved in promoting and operating the Lotto game. This also meant that the Chamber was unable to make any payments against the cost of the equipment for which it alone had assumed liability. Throughout this first year, the Chamber spent considerable sums of its own money to develop the game and keep it going. Indeed, developing and managing the Lotto became, for all intents and purposes, the BCCI's major — if not only — activity.

Having put up the developmental costs of setting up the Lotto game and even suffered the embarrassment of being sued by an advertising firm (and losing some of its assets in the process), the BCCI lost control of the management of the project towards the end of 1994, when the GoB suspended its operations and indicated its intention to award the management contract to another organisation. By this time, most of the Chamber's human and financial resources had been committed to the Lotto game, with the result that its developmental activities were almost non-existent. Finding a way to become financially sustainable had become more important than the programme of support for tourism, non-traditional exports, and business and trade promotion.

The moral of the story

The case of the BCCI provides one important lesson: sustainability is not about money! Pursuing so-called 'money-making' ventures can prove a dangerous distraction for many development agencies which are ill-equipped for the role. As the case study shows, both success and failure can have negative consequences. Success of an ancillary activity encourages programme managers to expand that activity and, in the process, to devote more time and resources to what, initially, was intended to be merely a secondary activity. Similarly, failure prompts programme managers to switch attention to the secondary activity, in order to ensure its success. Because there are often sunk costs and deep emotional commitment to the income-earning activity, it is difficult to withdraw from it once it has started. In either case, it is the original developmental objective that suffers.

Donors' insistence on sustainability in the purely financial sense must therefore be tempered by a recognition that desirable developmental activities — particularly those which cater to 'the poorest' — will never be(come) sustainable in that sense, because their capacity for revenue-generation is weak or non-existent (LaFond 1995; SIDA 1991,1995). As LaFond (1995) argues, it is time for donors to 'dispel the sustainability myth' by acknowledging the reality that, in most developing countries, there are constraints on local financing capacity which threaten sustainability.

On the recipient side, the overwhelming lesson is that sustainability is emphatically not a financial issue. There seems to be a common path down which recipient institutions travel. Having defined the problem posed by the termination of donor funding as a financial problem, they logically seek financial solutions. Halfway down that path, however, they find that they must confront the reality that sustainability means much more than simply finding a way to raise sufficient revenue from whatever source to meet their recurrent costs. If the definition of the problem is wrong, the solution must be equally wrong, because it will be founded on false premises. Moreover, where sustainability is equated with financial self-sufficiency, it is not always clear whether this means total or partial self-sufficiency.

Recipient institutions are thus well advised to agree from the outset an appropriate definition of sustainability which applies to their specific programmes and contexts, as well as a detailed plan for achieving it. In other words, a strategy for sustainability ought to be built into the programme design from inception, and the modalities for achieving it settled early in the life of the programme and not left to the final year (or worse, the dying months) of funding.

References

Belize Chamber of Commerce and Industry (1994) 'Impact, Funding Sources and Critical Factors Surrounding the Lotto Game', unpublished report, Belize City: BCCI.

Brinkerhoff, D. W. and A. A. Goldsmith (eds) (1990) *Institutional Sustainability in Agriculture and Rural Development: A Global Perspective*, New York: Praeger.

Brinkerhoff, D. W. (1992a) 'Looking out, looking ahead: guidelines for managing development programs', *International Review of Administrative Sciences*, 58: 483–503.

Brinkerhoff, D. W. (1992b) 'Promoting the sustainability of development institutions: a framework for strategy', *World Development*, 20(3): 369–83.

Brown, D. R. (1996) 'Learning and Institutional Sustainability in Donor Funded Development Programmes: Applying SCOPE to Three Caribbean Case Studies', PhD Dissertation, Institute for Development Policy and Management, University of Manchester.

Dichter, T. W. (1995) 'The Future of International NGOs in Microfinance', paper presented at a conference on Finance Against Poverty, University of Reading, UK.

Finsterbusch, K. (1990) 'Sustainability lessons: findings from cross-case analysis of seven development projects', in Brinkerhoff and Goldsmith (eds) 1990.

Gustafson, D. J. (1994) 'Developing sustainable institutions: lessons from cross-case analysis', *Public Administration and Development*, 14:121–34.

Hulme, D. and P. Mosley (1996) *Finance Against Poverty*, London and New York: Routledge.

LaFond, A. (1995) *Sustaining Primary Health Care*, London: Earthscan/Save the Children UK.

SIDA (1991) *The Art of Survival: A Study of Sustainability in Health Projects* (prepared by L. Andersson-Brolin *et al*), Stockholm: SIDA.

SIDA (1995) *Promoting Development by Proxy: An Evaluation of the Development Impact of Government Support to Swedish NGOs* (prepared by R. C. Riddell *et al*), Stockholm: SIDA.

USAID (1992) 'Evaluation of USAID–BCCI Project', unpublished report, Belize City: USAID.

The author

Deryck R Brown is currently a Research Associate of the Institute of Social and Economic Research (ISER) at the University of the West Indies (UWI). He was previously Director of the Trinidad & Tobago Small Business Development Company. This article first appeared in *Development in Practice*, Volume 7, Number 2, in 1997.

The wrong path: the World Bank's Country Assistance Strategy for Mexico

Carlos Heredia and Mary Purcell

Under the leadership of President James Wolfensohn at the World Bank, a greater emphasis has been placed on the Country Assistance Strategy (CAS) paper. This document lays out a strategy for the Bank's lending operations in a given country. It is updated every year for large countries like Mexico, and every two to three years for smaller countries.

According to Bank officials in Washington, even more importance will be placed on the CAS in Latin America in coming years. In a few countries in Africa and Asia, the process of developing the CAS has been opened up to include the opinions of some members of civil society. In Latin America, however, no CAS has been developed with public participation. Although the Bank's information policy does not require it to release the CAS, in many countries it has been circulated publicly. In Mexico, however, the CAS remains a secret document.

Among organisations of civil society, there are different opinions about the importance of the CAS in our work. Since it lays out the overall direction and objectives of Bank lending, its content is important to many groups seeking to influence Bank policies in their country. At the same time, however, it must be recognised that there is an important difference between what the CAS is supposed to be (a development strategy) and what it really is (a public-relations document geared to creditors).

In drafting the Mexico CAS, the Mexican Finance Secretariat called together representatives from the various Secretariats (Agriculture, Labour, Environment) and the government development banks for two weeks of meetings in which each Secretariat presented its analysis of the current situation, and its objectives for the upcoming year. This information was then incorporated into the CAS. No non-government entity participated in the process, nor did that idea ever emerge as a possibility.

When Equipo Pueblo requested a copy of the 1995 CAS (written in May that year), an official at the Mexico City Resident Mission of the World Bank (now called the Mexico Department) played down the importance of the document, saying that it would probably not be of much use to us. One week later, the same official sent word that the Bank would not give us a copy of the document. (We assumed that the government had something to do with the decision.) We then obtained the document through colleagues in Washington. But our experience illustrates the fact that policy changes and improved rhetoric issuing out of Washington have yet to trickle down to many Resident Missions. It also shows that the government has an important say in what information the Bank Missions will share. In fact, the new Operations Manager at the Bank's Mexico Department told us that they would be willing to initiate a participatory CAS as soon as the government agrees.

Content of the CAS: mistaken analysis and priorities

Given the nature of the process — one of government Secretariats emphasising their priorities — it is not surprising that the content of the 1995 Mexico CAS is highly disappointing. It uses the same outdated analysis to explain the economic crisis, and offers the same failed remedies, which we feel have proved incapable of addressing Mexico's structural impediments to development. Throughout the document, monetary issues are emphasised over social or economic issues. The Mexico CAS illustrates the misguided priorities of the Bank in countries throughout the world — sacrificing wages, jobs, and social services in order to pay the foreign debt and secure fiscal surpluses. According to Bank staff, Mexico was supposed to 'graduate' from the World Bank in the second half of the 1990s. Instead, it became the Bank's largest single borrower in 1995, and now accounts for 12 per cent of the Bank's total portfolio.

Here, we review some of the key sections of the 1995 CAS. Since it was written only five months after the eruption of the economic crisis, there was still a great deal of uncertainty regarding the overall Bank strategy. Thus, the Bank promises that the 1996 CAS (which was reportedly still being prepared in July 1996) will contain more information regarding the Bank's medium-term strategy in Mexico. In the future, we hope that Mexican civil society will be able to participate actively in developing the CAS, and not simply engage in *post facto* analysis of a secret document so central to the country's development strategy.

Causes of the crisis

The Mexico CAS does not even entertain the possibility that the economic strategy which the Bank has supported since 1982 may be partly to blame for the current crisis. Nowhere does the Bank accept any responsibility for flawed policy advice: everything is the fault of either government policy errors, political instability, or international volatility.

There is no serious review of the performance of the economic strategy — in other words,

structural adjustment — implemented since 1982. The Bank does not attempt to explain why, after 13 years of structural adjustment, average economic growth has been unable to keep up with the rate of population growth. While the Bank acknowledges (in retrospect) Mexico's over-dependence on short-term speculative capital, it does not answer the fundamental question of why Mexico is so extremely dependent on foreign capital flows to finance its current-account deficit: that is, what are the structural impediments to domestic savings?

Assessment of the economic programme

The Bank 'assesses' the Mexican government's programme as if it had nothing to do with developing it. Because of the relative size and importance of Mexico, the Bank is careful not to appear to be dictating policy. Nevertheless, it is clear that the Bank has played a key role in Mexico's adjustment programme and now in crisis management.

'Strengths'

According to the Bank, 'the program is based, correctly, on the premise that the immediate problem is largely one of short-term cash-flow, and not of insolvency, and so its first objective is to restore stability by re-building international confidence'. We disagree with that analysis, believing that there is solid evidence — in the financial and productive sectors — that the crisis is of a structural nature, and that only the tens of billions of dollars in foreign loans have allowed a temporary respite from a massive insolvency crisis.

The Bank and the government of Mexico continue to count on exports 'to lead a recovery of economic growth'. They highlight the more 'competitive' — devalued — peso as a key reason for such an export boom. They do not, however, address the other factors pointing to the temporary nature of the surge in exports. The vast majority of companies which have increased their sales abroad are doing so because of a severely depressed domestic market, and not because they have increased their output. As the peso slowly becomes over-valued, and as the government induces a (minor) recovery through public spending in the run-up to the 1997 mid-term federal elections, exports will lose their momentum.

Risks

The Bank recognises that 'the clearest risk to the economic program concerns the banking sector, which is under systemic stress due to the crisis'. The fact that in late 1995 the two most important banks in Mexico (Banamex and Bancomer) had to rely on public subsidies is indicative of the severity of the solvency crisis shared by most economic actors in the country.

The Bank's strategy for dealing with the banking crisis is to provide over one billion dollars to bolster the banks, instead of addressing the inability of seven million debtors to service their debts. Unless the economic situation of indebted businesses and families improves, however, the banks will face an increasing problem of non-performing loans.

The second key risk pointed out by the Bank is 'the social costs of the crisis, which is already causing widespread transitional unemployment'. Along with debt, this is probably the most serious problem facing Mexico today. Close to two million people (instead of the one million estimated by the government and the Bank) lost their jobs in 1995. Indeed, surveys show that, even if their economic situation improves, many of the firms which laid workers off are not planning to re-hire them in the future. Thus, unemployment appears to be more than a transitional problem.

Mexico's development objectives and policies

The CAS devotes only two pages out of 22 to this subject, one of which focuses solely on private-sector development. One short paragraph is dedicated to the theme of poverty-alleviation, and another to environmental sustainability. Both are more descriptive of existing problems than strategy-oriented. Although the phrase 'poverty reduction' is used several times, there

is never a mention of any sort of comprehensive strategy to achieve this. The government has not fulfilled its commitment to develop a National Poverty Eradication Plan, made at the 1995 Copenhagen Social Summit. Concepts such as social equity, gender equality, and income-generation for the poor are completely absent from the Mexico CAS.

The Bank's ever-present assumption that a more rapid pace in economic growth in and of itself allows for a reduction in poverty has been proved wrong many times. Mexico's levels of absolute poverty and inequality have increased steadily since 1982 (with the possible exception of 1990–91), and the 1994–96 crisis has exacerbated poverty in a serious way. According to a recent World Bank study, 85 per cent of the Mexican population now lives in poverty. Prior experience suggests that geographical targeting of resources where poor and indigenous people are concentrated is not enough for programmes to reach those most in need.

Designing an effective development strategy for Mexico

The World Bank's 1995 Country Assistance Strategy for Mexico is highly disappointing. Both its content and the process by which it was developed illustrate the enormous gap between the needs and realities of millions of Mexicans and the policy recommendations of the government and its World Bank advisers. A truly effective assistance strategy for Mexico would prioritise innovative approaches to development that included income-generating strategies for the poor, direct access to subsidised credit for small and medium-sized producers and businesses (focusing especially on women), and concrete measures for de-centralising economic and political power. It should also set goals: for example, for the gradual elimination of poverty and the creation of jobs. None of these issues is significantly addressed in the 1995 CAS.

While macro-economic management is clearly crucial, it cannot take the place of real development initiatives. A one-billion dollar social safety-net to 'protect' the poor from the economic crisis does not constitute a poverty-eradication strategy. A sustainable development programme must be developed with the participation of organisations of civil society — including producer groups, non-government organisations (NGOs), labour unions, academics, and so on. Equipo Pueblo has joined with others to launch a campaign to ensure greater access to information, and the right to participate in World Bank and Inter-American Development Bank projects and policies in Mexico. Part of our work will be to push both the Bank and the government for public involvement in developing the World Bank's Country Assistance Strategy.

The authors

Mary Purcell and Carlos Heredia work with Equipo Pueblo, a Mexican NGO involved in policy analysis and related lobbying. This paper, based on their July 1996 report 'The World Bank's Country Assistance Strategy for Mexico: Analysis and an Alternative Agenda', appeared in the July–August 1996 issue of *The Other Side of Mexico* (No 47), and has been reproduced here with permission. Its first appearance in *Development in Practice* was in Volume 7, Number 2, in 1997.

Annotated bibliography

This Bibliography represents a sample of agnostic, unorthodox, or even heretical thinking about the nature and purpose of development, particularly concerning relations among nations and peoples. In an effort to reflect something of the richness and diversity of such thinking, we have included several edited collections, as well as works by authors who have come to be icons or touchstones of critical alternatives to mainstream analysis. The Bibliography was compiled and annotated by Deborah Eade and Caroline Knowles, Editor and Reviews Editor respectively of Development in Practice.

Books

Nassau A. Adams: *Worlds Apart: The North–South Divide and the International System*
London: Zed Books, 1993
Traces the history of North-South relations since 1945, focusing on the role of the international economic system. Relates the efforts of the South to change a system it considered unjust and inimical to its interests; the partial successes achieved in the 1960s and 70s (including the creation of UNCTAD), and subsequent reversals; the metamorphosis of the IMF and World Bank into the principal vehicles for the conduct of the North's relations with the South. Describes the current impasse wherein the South must accept policy prescriptions dictated by the North, yet can look forward to little real prospect of increasing living standards, let alone narrowing the North-South gap.

Samir Amin: *Maldevelopment: Anatomy of a Global Failure*
London: Zed Books (with the UN University and the Third World Forum) 1990
Analyses the failure of development from a political standpoint, aiming to integrate economic, political, social and cultural considerations and fit them into a local framework that takes account of interaction on a world scale. Amin then offers a thesis of 'alternative development', which would be national and popular, and favour South–South cooperation through a polycentric world system which would replace the five 'great powers' (USA, USSR, Europe, Japan, China) and the duopoly of two superpowers which marginalises the Third World, and provide it with real scope for development.

Augusto Boal: *Theater of the Oppressed*
London: Pluto Press (originally published in 1974 as *Teatro de Oprimido*), 1979
Traces the history of drama since the ancient Greeks to argue that all theatre is necessarily political. Theatre used to be of and for the people — singing and dancing in the open air — but was slowly taken over by the ruling classes, so changing the concept of theatre to feature actors (protagonists) and a passive audience. Using examples from Brazil, the author argues that radical theatre in Latin America is breaking down the barriers between actors and spectators. All must act and all must be protagonists in the necessary transformation of society.

Rosi Braidotti *et al: Women, the Environment and Sustainable Development: Towards a Theoretical Synthesis*
London: Zed Books, 1994
An attempt to disentangle the various positions on sustainable development, the environment, and women and to clarify the political and theoretical issues at stake. Offers a critical review of issues such as the feminist analysis of science itself and the power relations inherent in the production of knowledge; women, environment, and development (WED); alternative development; environmental reformism; and deep ecology, social ecology, and ecofeminism. The authors also present their own ideas on the basic elements necessary in constructing a paradigmatic shift — emphasising such values as holism, mutuality, justice, autonomy, self-reliance, sustainability, and peace.

Cristovam Buarque: *The End of Economics? Ethics and the Disorder of Progress*
London: Zed Books, 1993 (originally published in Brazil as *A Desordem do Progresso: O fim de era dos economistas e a construcao do futuro*, 1990)
Presents the case for an ethical system to guide economic theory and practice, arguing that high levels of consumption among the rich cannot be sustained and extended to the entire population. This implies a stark choice between a brand of development geared to universal consumption and technology, building on a system of social partitioning on a global scale; or the challenge of building a new order in which the economic system is governed by ethical principles, a framework in which respect for nature and abolition of human want would be the key social objectives. Technological advance must respect nature, and the fetish of applying economic theories without regard to their human consequences must be abandoned.

Raff Carmen: *Autonomous Development: Humanising the Landscape — An Excursion into Radical Thinking and Practice*
London: Zed Books, 1996
Arguing that development is primarily an act of human creation, the author affirms that people are silenced by human agency, not by divine ordinance. The decolonisation of the mind is what permits constructive change: subjugation is as much the key to the 'over-development' of the North as to the 'under-development' of the South. Rejecting conventional approaches which start by analysing what people lack, Carmen focuses on the 'cultural, social, educational, ethical and other values' that characterise them; and in which human development must necessarily be embedded.

Robert Chambers: *Whose Reality Counts: Putting the First Last*
London: IT Publications, 1997
This sequel to *Rural Development: Putting the Last First* (1983) argues that central issues in development have been overlooked and that many errors have flowed from domination by those with power. Development professionals need new approaches and methods for interacting, learning, and knowing. Through analysing experience of past mistakes and myths, and the continuing methodological evolution of PRA, the author points towards solutions. Rural and urban people alike express and analyse their local, complex, and diverse realities in ways which are often at odds with the top–down realities imposed by professionals. Personal, professional, and institutional change is necessary if the realities of the poor are to receive greater recognition.

Noam Chomsky: *World Orders, Old and New*
London: Pluto, 1994
An acclaimed scholar of linguistics, Chomsky is more widely known as a relentless critic of all forms of contemporary imperialism, and of US foreign policy in particular. Common to Chomsky's prolific output is a concern with human rights, and with exposing the negative global impact of Western notions of liberal democracy in the context of its defence of corporate power, of which this book is a recent example.

Michel Chossudovsky: *The Globalisation of Poverty: Impacts of IMF and World Bank Reforms*
London: Zed Books with Third World Network, 1997
Shows how the structures of the global economy have changed since the early 1980s and explains

how the World Bank and IMF have forced Third World (and, since 1989, Eastern European countries) to facilitate these changes. Describes the consequences of a new financial order which feeds on human poverty and destruction of the environment, generates social apartheid, encourages racism and ethnic strife, and undermines the rights of women. The result is the globalisation of poverty.

Jonathan Crush (ed.): *Power of Development*
London: Routledge, 1995
Post-colonial, post-modern, and feminist thinking have focused on the power structures embedded within the discourse and practice of development. Rather than asking 'what development is, or is not, or how it can be more accurately defined, better "theorised", or sustainably practised', these 20 essays examine the language of development — 'the forms in which it makes its arguments and establishes its authority, the manner in which it constructs the world'. Contributors variously show that although development is itself a Western myth about the world, it has come to assume a kind of global reality of its own — however distant from that of the people and societies it describes.

Arturo Escobar: *Encountering Development: The Making and Unmaking of the Third World*
Princeton: Princeton University Press, 1995
Suggests that the idea of development, and even the Third World, may be in the process of being unmade, because of the failure of development and increasing opposition in the South. Escobar examines the discourse and apparatus of development since 1949, and the construction of the notion of 'under-development' in economic theories. Using examples from Colombia, he demonstrates the ways in which the apparatus functions through the systematic production of knowledge and power in fields such as rural development, sustainable development, and women and development. The conclusion deals with how to imagine a post-development regime of representation, and how to investigate and pursue alternatives in contemporary social movements in the Third World.

Franz Fanon: *The Wretched of the Earth*,
Harmondsworth: Penguin Books, 1963
(originally published in French as *Les damnés de la terre*, 1961)
An impassioned critique of colonialism in all its expressions, and a rallying cry for the emancipation of 'the wretched of the earth', this classic has influenced many liberation movements. Here, as in his earlier work, *Black Skins, White Masks* (first published in 1952 as *Peau Noire, Masques Blancs*), Fanon argues that cultural alienation and internalised assumptions of inferiority and Otherness are the inevitable corollary to the condition of subjugation. The process of decolonisation is necessarily a violent phenomenon: it is no less than the dissolution of both coloniser and colonised, in terms both of national histories and of people's lived experiences.

Paulo Freire: *Pedagogy of the Oppressed*,
Harmondsworth: Penguin Books, 1972
(originally published in Portuguese as *Pedagogia del Oprimido*)
Defining reading as a political act, the author presents a theory of adult education based on communication and problem-solving dialogue between equals. Literacy and liberation are joined in the notion of 'naming the world', the basis upon which people who are poor and oppressed can mobilise to change it. Freire was a prolific writer, though this remains his best-known work. Other major titles include: *Education for Critical Consciousness*; *Cultural Action for Freedom*, *Education for Critical Consciousness*; *The Politics of Education: Culture, Power and Liberation*; *Learning to Question: A Pedagogy of Liberation*; and (with Peter McLaren) *Critical Pedagogy and Predatory Culture: Oppositional Politics in a Post-Modern Era*.

Denis Goulet: *Development Ethics:*
A Guide to Theory and Practice
London: Zed Books, 1995
An introductory guide to development ethics which aims to question the nature of development and its declared goals. The author formulates general principles underlying ethical strategies in development, and discusses their

application in such topics as technology for development, ecology and ethics, culture and tradition, and the ethics of aid.

Gustavo Gutiérrez: *The Power of the Poor in History: Selected Writings*
Maryknoll: Orbis Books, 1993
Eight selected texts from the ten years following publication of the classic *Theology of Liberation*. The first presents a biblical survey of some of the major sources of liberation theology, followed by three articles which were milestones in its evolution: 'Involvement in the Liberation Process'; 'Liberation Praxis and Christian Faith'; and 'The Historical Power of the Poor'. The third section represents Gutiérrez' reaction to the Latin America Bishops' Conference in 1979, at which they tried to distance themselves liberation theology. The final section illustrates his attempts to reach out to people outside Latin America, in which he argues that it is necessary for everyone to learn to see the world 'from below' (the 'Theology from the Underside of History').

Kofi Buenor Hadjor:
Dictionary of Third World Terms
London: I.B. Tauris, 1992
Words associated with the Third World are often loaded with assumptions and cultural attitudes, and may mean quite different things to people in different parts of the world. This dictionary focuses on this complex vocabulary. The author gives not only the meaning but also the background of the terms defined, drawing on many disciplines including economics, politics, sociology, anthropology, and gender studies. Entries range from short factual definitions to in-depth essays on key concepts such as dependency theory, liberation theology, or Malthusianism.

Cees Hamelink: *World Communication: Disempowerment and Self-empowerment*
London: Zed Books and Penang: Southbound/Third World Network, 1995
A critical examination of the role of the media in treating information as a commodity, and of transnational corporations in manipulating developments in information and communication technology for their own profit. The author

traces the links between human rights — particularly political and cultural rights — and shows how rights and citizenship can be suppressed or enhanced through global communication.

Cynthia Hewitt de Alcántara (ed): *Social Futures, Global Visions*
Oxford: Blackwell with UNRISD, 1996
A collection of papers from a conference organised by UNRISD to coincide with the World Summit for Social Development in 1995 to reflect on the processes currently driving social change. The scale and speed of change have rendered existing paradigms and models inadequate to understand the nature of contemporary social dilemmas, and new thinking is required to provide more appropriate conceptual and institutional frameworks for coping with escalating social problems. The essays attempt to interpret and illuminate the social changes ushered in by the forces of globalisation, and the impact of these forces on human welfare and solidarity.

Ivan Illich: *In the Mirror of the Past: Lectures and Addresses 1978–90*
London: Marion Boyars, 1992
A collection of notes from lectures and public meetings, serving as an introduction to the work of Illich, radical author of famous critiques of the educational and medical professions. Illich suggests that only by reflecting on the past is it possible to recognise the radical 'otherness' of late-20th century assumptions and become aware of the hidden orthodoxies. This collection introduces Illich's ideas on peace and development, culture and history, the alternative to economics, literacy and language.

Naila Kabeer: *Reversed Realities: Gender Hierarchies in Development Thought*
London: Verso, 1994
Traces the emergence of 'women' as a specific category in development thought and examines alternative frameworks for analysing gender hierarchies. The household is identified as a primary site for the construction of power relations; the extent to which gender inequalities are revealed in different approaches to the

concept of the family unit is studied. The inadequacies of the poverty line as a measuring tool are assessed, and an overview of the issue of population policies is given.

Rajni Kothari: *Poverty: Human Consciousness and the Amnesia of Development*
London: Zed Books, 1995
Explores the meanings of poverty in its economic, social, and political aspects and analyses the roles of the State and the market, both nationally and internationally in the deepening of poverty. Also examines the phenomenon of disem-powerment and the declining access of the poor to the power structures of society.

Serge Latouche: *In the Wake of the Affluent Society: An Exploration of Post-development*
London: Zed Books, 1993
Argues that all development is a process of Westernisation which, in reality, has become a one-dimensional preoccupation with material standards of living. However there is little prospect of most of humanity reaching Western levels of consumption, and this reconstruction of societies in a Western ideological mould does not fit the Third World. The failure of development and its impossibility as a global idea is seen as much in the alienation of the cities of the North as in the shanty towns and wrecked villages of the South. Latouche finds hope in the response of the poor, fighting for survival in the 'informal sector': synthesising modernity and tradition, he develops an alternative model of society.

John Martinussen: *Society, State and Market: A Guide to Competing Theories of Development*
London: Zed Books, 1997
A multi-disciplinary account of how development theory has evolved since 1945, raising questions about the nature of development theory and the differentiated nature of countries in the South. The book presents a full range of theoretical approaches and current debates, organised around four themes: economic development and underdevelopment; politics and the State; socio-economic development and the State; civil society and the development process.

Manfred A. Max-Neef: *From the Outside Looking In: Experiences in 'Barefoot' Economics*
London: Zed Books, 1992
This has become a minor classic since it was first issued by the Dag Hammarskjöld Foundation in 1982. The author relates and reflects on two experiences in 'bare-foot economics' — economics as if people mattered, in which 'the poor must learn to circumvent the national (economic) system'. The first is about the indian and black peasants in Ecuador, and the second about artisans in Brazil — one the story of a success that failed; the other a failure that succeeded. Both refer to a people's quest for self-reliance and are lessons in economics practised on a human scale, in which human facts and feelings replace abstract statistics. These ideas are explored further in *Human Scale Development: Conception, Application and Further Reflections* (1991).

Ozay Mehmet: *Westernising the Third World: The Eurocentricity of Economic Development Theories*
London: Routledge, 1995
The author blames the failure of Third World development on Western theories and prescriptions. He identifies the mainstream economic theories and demonstrates that they are Eurocentric and unsuitable for the Third World. He also examines both Classical theories of economic development and their post-war Neo-Classical counterparts, arguing that these are fundamentally flawed because of their subjective and normative assumptions. Further chapters discuss model-building and macro-planning and the New Economic Order. The book concludes with an appraisal of the current situation and an examination of the future agenda for development studies.

Maria Mies and Vandana Shiva:
Ecofeminism: A Feminist and Ecological Reader on Biotechnology
London: Zed Books, 1993
An analysis of environmental, development, and feminist issues from a unique North–South perspective. The authors review prevailing economic theories, conventional concepts of women's emancipation, the myth of 'catching up' development, the philosophical foundations

of modern science and technology, and the omission of ethics when discussing such issues as advances in reproductive technology and biotechnology. In constructing their own epistemology and methodology, they look to the potential of movements advocating consumer liberation and subsistence production, sustainability, and regeneration; and they argue for an acceptance of limits and reciprocity, and a rejection of exploitation, the endless commoditisation of needs, and violence.

Julius Nyerere: *Freedom and Development: A Selection from Writings and Speeches 1968–73*
Dar Es Salaam: Oxford University Press, 1973
The third major collection of former President Julius Nyerere's speeches and writings, from 1968 to 1973. Like the previous volumes (*Freedom and Unity* and *Freedom and Socialism*), it is a representative sample of his views on socialism, economic policy, human equality, African unity and liberation, and international relations.

Charles P. Oman and Ganeshan Wignaraja:
The Post-war Evolution of Development Thinking
London: Macmillan with the OECD Development Centre, 1991
Development thinking and practice are in a state of flux — theory apparently offering little by way of solution to the crisis. This book provides a critical survey of the different schools of development thought in which both orthodox and alternative schools of thought are covered in an up-to-date and non-technical manner.

Md Anisur Rahman: *People's Self-development: Perspectives on Participatory Action Research — A Journey through Experience*
London: Zed Books, 1993
A collection of articles and previously published papers in which the author reflects on development through collective local initiatives by people themselves — and how to promote such development. This thinking has grown out of his long involvement in popular initiatives, experimentation with participatory research, and experience of field 'animation' work and training of 'animators' in Asia and Africa. Some of the key ideas centre on what the notion of self-reliance should actually mean; an approach to Participatory Action Research (PAR) in terms of the self-emancipation of the popular classes; the importance of knowledge relations as a factor which can perpetuate domination over ordinary people; and an examination of popular knowledge.

Majid Rahnema with Victoria Bawtree (eds):
The Post-development Reader
London: Zed Books, 1997
A collection of essays by over 40 thinkers and activists who evaluate the dominant development paradigm and what it has done to the peoples of the world and their diverse and sustainable ways of living. They also present some of the experiences and ideas out of which people are trying to construct their more humane and culturally and ecologically respectful alternatives to development.

Wolfgang Sachs (ed.): *The Development Dictionary: A Guide to Knowledge as Power*
London: Zed Books, 1992
A collection of essays covering some of the key ideas of the development discourse in which each concept is examined from a historical and anthropological perspective. The chapters identify the shifting role played by each concept in the debate on development since 1945, demonstrate how each concept filters perception, highlighting certain aspects of reality while excluding others, and show how this bias is rooted in particular civilisational attitudes adopted during the course of European history. Each chapter offers a different way of looking at the world and a glimpse of the riches which survive in non-Western cultures in spite of development.

Edward Said: *Culture and Imperialism*
London: Vintage Books, 1994
Develops arguments presented in *Orientalism*, Said's critique of Western attitudes towards the East, focusing on a general worldwide pattern of imperial culture, and a historical experience of resistance against empire. Said examines the ways in which Western literature has represented oppressed people, and influenced

the fight for equality and human community. He also discusses 'culture' and the difficulties in reconciling the cruelty of colonialist and racist oppression with the cultural expressions of societies that engage in those practices. One of imperialism's achievements was to bring the world much closer together, and although in that process the separation between Europeans and 'natives' was insidious and unjust, the historical experience of empire is a common one.

Jeremy Seabrook: *Pioneers of Change: Experiments in Creating a Humane Society*
London: Zed Books, 1993
Describes individuals and movements worldwide who are seeking to develop new visions of society and experiment in practical ways with new lifestyles, new paths of development, and new relations with Nature. All share a belief in the value of diversity — genetic, cultural, and individual — and challenge the dominant consumerist world view. All have been recipients of the Right Livelihood Award, widely known as the Alternative Nobel Prize, which is presented in recognition of pioneering efforts in the areas of peace, sustainable development, environmental integrity, social justice, and human rights.

Gita Sen and Caren Grown: *Development, Crises and Alternative Visions: Third World Women's Perspectives*
New York: Monthly Review Press, 1987
A brief introduction to development economics, written from Southern feminist perspectives, which examines why strategies designed to achieve overall economic growth and increased industrial and agricultural productivity have proven to be harmful to women. Women's contributions are central to the ability of households, communities, and nations to survive, and a much-needed reorientation of development analysis can be achieved by starting from the perspective of poor women.

Naresh Singh and Vangile Titi (eds):
Empowerment: Towards Sustainable Development
London: Zed Books with IISD, 1995
Explores ways to move towards a concept and practice of development that integrates the needs of people, the economy, the environment, and the practical world of decision-making. It argues that poverty alleviation and sustainable development are only likely if empowerment and its practical institutionalisation in the law, the educational process, and the machinery of government becomes a reality.

Rehman Sobhan: *Agrarian Reform and Social Transformation: Preconditions for Development*
London: Zed Books, 1993
Focusing attention on agrarian reform as a tool for eradicating rural poverty, the author discusses experiences of agrarian reform throughout the South, building a typology of such reforms, the varying socio-political circumstances in which they were enacted, and how this influenced their outcome. He concludes that only those countries where rural poverty was ameliorated rapidly and the foundations laid for permanent, all-round development had carried out comprehensive, egalitarian agrarian reforms. This applies as much to market-oriented countries like Japan, South Korea and Taiwan, as to socialist China or Cuba.

The South Centre: *Facing the Challenge: Responses to the Report of the South Commission*
London: Zed Books with The South Centre, 1993
The Challenge to the South — the 1990 Report of the South Commission — offered a detailed analysis of the problems facing the countries of the South. This book is a companion volume of 33 commentaries on the Report, corresponding to the South Commission's wish to supplement and expand its work through public comment and debate. It contains a summary of the Report itself, and includes essays by leading intellectuals and activists, as well as senior IMF and World Bank officials.

Ngugi wa Thiong'o: *Decolonising the Mind: The Politics of Language in African Literature*
London: James Currey with Heinemann Kenya, 1986
One of the most important contemporary African novelists argues that the politics of language in African literature is about national, democratic, and human liberation. The choice of language and the use to which it is put is central

to people's definition of themselves in relation to the natural and social environment. Shows how language was used as a means of oppression under colonial rule, and calls for the search for the African novel and African drama as a way of liberating the people and expressing their lives in literature.

The World: A Third World Guide
Montevideo: The Third World Institute (biennial)
A country-by-country compendium of history, society, and politics written from a range of Southern perspectives. It contains global and national maps with illustrated graphs and statistics, and in-depth description of key global issues such as childhood, women, food, health, education, population, employment, habitat, human welfare.

Immanuel Wallerstein: *After Liberalism*
New York: New Press, 1995
Examines the process of disintegration of the modern world-system following the dissolution of the USSR, and speculates on the changes that may occur during the next few decades. The author argues that rather than this representing the triumph of liberalism over communism, liberal reformism is also being rejected, because its policies worsen rather than improve the economic situation of the majority of the population. He believes we are now entering into a world 'after liberalism'. He explores the historical choices available and suggests paths for reconstructing the world-system on a more rational and equitable basis.

Ponna Wignaraja (ed.): *New Social Movements in the South: Empowering the People*
London: Zed Books, 1993
Papers by scholars from the UN University's Third World and Development Project seeking alternatives to Western paradigms of development and democratic notions and institutions. The book identifies various social movements and people's responses to a range of crises and shows how such new responses also attempt to protect the South from penetration by external forces which further intensify these internal tensions. Popular responses are taking the form of new social movements, people's movements, and experiments, and this book examines several which have elements of sustainability and which promote development and democracy in new terms. The book thus provides an overview of the new thinking that is emerging under different socio-political circumstances.

Marshall Wolfe: *Elusive Development*
London: Zed Books, 1996
A critical overview of the policies and trends emanating from post-war thinking and practice in development, particularly at the inter-governmental level. Drawing on a long and intimate knowledge of the UN system, and of competing influences upon it (scholarly, political, and practical), the author dissects the myths and vague theories that 'development' has espoused. A valuable guide to the background behind concepts that still shape today's thinking; and a sceptical view of the doomed quest for a universal recipe for development.

Other resources

Convergence/Convergencia
Editor: Karen Yarmol-Franko
Published quarterly by the International Council for Adult Education (ICAE)
(ISSN:0010-8146)
A global journal of adult education that addresses issues, practices and developments in the broad field of adult and non-formal education; reports on current developments; and acts as a network for the 100 national, regional and sectoral members of ICAE worldwide. Articles are published in English, French, and Spanish.

Cultures and Development
Editor: Thierry Verhelst
Published three times per year by the South-North Network Cultures and Development
(ISSN: 1370-0057)
Focuses on the role of local cultures in social life and in 'development' in both South and North. Aims to present the Network's research projects and to be a guide to concepts and methods for social activists, development practitioners, and academics.

DAWN (Development Alternatives with Women for a New Era)

A worldwide network of Southern feminist thinkers and activists, involved in research, training, communications, and publications as well as advocacy work from the grassroots to international policy making. Its members believe that feminism is about transformational politics, and so must address all of the structures of oppression and domination which shape women's lives, including racism, class, and nationality. See **Sen and Grown** (1987) for an account of DAWN's vision and purpose.

Development

Editor: Wendy Harcourt

Published quarterly by Sage on behalf of the Society for International Development (ISSN 1011-6370)

Aims to be a point of reference for the dialogue between activists and intellectuals committed to the search for alternative paths of social transformation towards a more sustainable and just world. In particular, it seeks to bring in local and innovative perspectives from the margins of the global development discourse; and to bring accountability, equity, and democracy to development.

Development Dialogue

Editors: Sven Hamrell and Olle Nordberg

Published twice-yearly (ISSN 0345-2328)

A journal of international development cooperation published by the Dag Hammarskjöld Foundation, within the framework of its seminars and conferences on the social, economic, legal and cultural issues facing the Third World. From the mid-1970s, it became a vehicle for the 'Another Development' school of thought associated with Marc Nerfin and Manfred Max-Neef. It has since published a number of influential guest-edited issues, for instance on the reform of the UN system.

Development in Practice

Editor: Deborah Eade

Published quarterly by Oxfam (UK and Ireland) (ISSN 0961-4524)

A forum for practitioners, policy makers, and academics to exchange information and analysis concerning the social dimensions of development and humanitarian relief. As a multidisciplinary journal of policy and practice, *Development in Practice* reflects a wide range of institutional and cultural backgrounds and a variety of professional expertise.

Organisations

El Taller is a global NGO think-tank concerned to support people's initiatives aiming at economic, political, and ideological empowerment of the disenfranchised towards reducing dependence and promoting greater understanding between the people of the world. **El Taller** organises workshops and other events and produces occasional publications.

IRED (Innovations et réseaux pour le développement) is a global network of individuals and organisations that aims to promote forms of local and global development which answer people's needs and also foster their participation in strengthening and democratising civil society. It offers technical support in the fields of management, training, alternative financing, and appropriate technology. IRED's quarterly bulletin, *IRED Forum*, is available in English, French, and Spanish.

People-Centred Development Forum is an international alliance of individuals and organisations dedicated to the creation of just, inclusive, and sustainable human societies through voluntary citizen action. Its Founding Director is David Korten, author of the influential books *Getting to the Twenty-first Century: Voluntary Action and the Global Agenda* (1990) and *When Corporations Rule the World* (1995). The Forum's numerous information activities all reinforce and elaborate a basic message that transformational change to substantially reduce current levels of inequality and exploitation is not only possible, it has become essential to human survival. For further information and a list of publications see the Forum's website: http://iisd1.iisd.ca/pcdf/

SID (Society for International Development) is an international network of academics, activists,

NGOs and policy-makers with local Chapters in 40 countries and members in most nations. Its overall purpose is to promote social changes that will create a world that is more people-centred, sustainable, democratic, just, and inclusive. Its two main aims are to catalyse civil society as a means of defending rights and monitoring the actions of the state and the private sector; and to build bridges between the practice and theory of development. See also **SID**'s quarterly journal, *Development*.

South Centre is a new, permanent inter-government organisation of developing countries, which grew out of the work of the South Commission. In promoting Southern solidarity, South–South co-operation, and coordinated participation by developing countries in international forums, the South Centre has full intellectual independence. It enjoys support and cooperation from the governments of Southern countries and is in regular working contact with the Non-Aligned Movement and the Group of 77. The South Centre prepares and disseminates information (including a regular briefing, *Southletter*), analysis, and recommendations on international economic, social and political matters of concern to the South.

The Third World Network is an international network of organisations and individuals involved in issues relating to development, Third World, and North–South affairs. Its objectives are to conduct research on economic, social, and environmental issues pertaining to the South; to organise and participate in seminars; and to provide a platform representing broadly Southern perspectives in international forums. **TWN** publishes a wide range of books as well as the daily *SUNS (South–North Development Monitor)*; *Third World Economics*; and the monthly magazine *Third World Resurgence* (an African edition, *African Agenda,* is published by Africa Secretariat of TWN; and a Spanish-language edition, *Sur,* is published by the Third World Institute).

The Transnational Institute (TNI) was founded in 1973 to address the disparity between rich and poor peoples and nations of the world, investigate its causes, and develop alternatives for its remedy. An independent fellowship of researchers and activists worldwide are working in three main areas: global economy, peace and security, and democratisation. Recent publications (all co-published with Pluto Press) include John Cavanagh, Daphne Wysham and Marcos Arruda (eds): *Beyond Bretton Woods: Alternatives to the Global Economic Order*, Susan George: *The Debt Boomerang: How Third World Debt Harms Us All*, Walden Bello *et al.*: *Dark Victory: The United States, Structural Adjustment and Global Poverty*; and David Sogge (ed): *Compassion and Calculation: The Business of Private Foreign Aid*.

UNESCO promotes collaboration among nations through education, science, culture, and communication. Its main goals are those of universal basic education, and Education for the Twenty-First Century. UNESCO also sponsors a wide range of programmes within the cultural sphere, such as the World Decade for Cultural Development (1988–1997), which has promoted research and exchange programmes geared to enhance the recognition of the cultural and environmental dimensions of development. The report of the World Commission on Culture and Development, *Our Creative Diversity*, was published in 1995. UNESCO has a vast publishing programme, including *UNESCO Courier*, a monthly magazine on issues of topical interest produced in 36 languages and in Braille; *UNESCO Sources*, a monthly update on the organisation's activities, also produced in five languages and free of charge; and the annual *World Education Report* and *World Communication Report*. UNESCO hosts a website at: http://www.education.unesco.org/

Addresses of publishers and relevant organisations

Blackwell Publishers, 108 Cowley Road, Oxford OX4 1JF, UK. Fax: +44 (1865) 791347.

Marion Boyars Publishers, 24 Lacy Road, London SW15 1NL, UK. Fax: +44 (181) 789 8122.

Carfax Publishing, PO Box 25, Abingdon OX14 3UE, UK. Fax: +44 (1235) 401550.

James Currey Publishers, 73 Botley Road, Oxford OX2 0BS, UK. Fax: +44 (1865) 246454.

Dag Hammarskjöld Foundation, övre Slottsgarten 2, 75220 Uppsala, Sweden.

DAWN, c/o Women and Development Unit, University of West Indies, School of Continuing Studies, Pinelands, St Michael, Barbados, West Indies. Fax: +1 (809) 426 3006.

Earthscan Publications, 120 Pentonville Road, London N1 9JN, UK. Fax: +44 (171) 278 1142.

Heinemann Kenya, Kijabe Street, PO Box 45314, Nairobi, Kenya.

I. B. Tauris Publishers, Victoria House, Bloomsbury Square, London WC1B 4DZ, UK. Fax: +44 (171) 916 1068.

IRED, 3 rue de Varembé, Case 116, 1211 Geneva 20, Switzerland. Fax: +41 (22) 740 0011.

Intermediate Technology Publications, 103–105 Southampton Row, London WC1B 4HH, UK. Fax: +44 (171) 436 2013.

International Council for Adult Education, 720 Bathurst Street, Toronto, Ontario M5S 2R4, Canada.

International Development Research Centre, 250 Albert Street, PO Box 8500, Ottawa, Ontario, Canada K1G 3H9.

International Institute for Sustainable Development, 161 Portage Avenue, Winnipeg, Manitoba R3B 0Y4, Canada. Fax: +1 (204) 958 7710

Macmillan Press, Houndmills, Basingstoke RG21 6XS, UK. Fax: +44 (1256) 842084.

Monthly Review Press, 122 West 27th Street, New York NY 10001, USA. Fax: +1 (212) 727 3676.

The New Press, 450 West 41st Street, New York NY 10036, USA. Fax: +1 (212) 268 6349.

Orbis Books, Box 302, NY 10545-0302, USA. Fax: +1 (914) 941 7005.

OECD, 2 rue André Pascal, 75775 Paris, Cedex 16, France. Fax: +33 (1) 452 47943.

Oxfam Publications, Oxfam UK and Ireland, 274 Banbury Road, Oxford OX2 7DZ, UK. Fax: +44 (1865) 313925.

Oxford University Press, Walton Street, Oxford OX2 6DP, UK. Fax: +44 (1865) 56646.

Penguin Books, Bath Road, Harmondsworth, Middlesex UB7 0DA, UK. Fax: +44 (181) 899 4099.

People-Centred Development Forum, 14E 17th Street, Suite 5, New York NY 10003, USA. Fax: +1 (212) 242 1901.

Pluto Press, 345 Archway Road, London N6 5AA, UK. Fax: +44 (181) 348 9133.

Princeton University Press, 41 William Street, Princeton, New Jersey NJ 08540, USA. Fax: +1 (609) 258 6305.

Routledge, 11 New Fetter Lane, London EC4P 4EE, UK. Fax: +44 (171) 842 2302.

Sage Publications, 6 Bonhill Street, London EC2A 4PU, UK. Fax: +44 (171) 374 8741.

Society for International Development, 207 via Panisperna, 00184 Rome, Italy. Fax: +39 (6) 487 2170.

South Centre, Chemin du Champ-d'Anier 17, Case Postale 228, 1211 Geneva 19, Switzerland. Fax: +41 (22) 798 3433. Also South Centre, PO Box 71000, Dar-es-Salaam, Tanzania. Fax: +255 (51) 46146.

South-North Network Cultures and Development, rue Joseph II straat 174, 1000 Brussels, Belgium. Fax: +32 (2) 231 1413.

Southbound Sdn. Bhd., 9 College Square, 10250 Penang, Malaysia. Fax: +60 (4) 228 1758.

Third World Network, International Secretariat, 228 Macallister Road, 10400 Penang, Malaysia. Fax: +60 (4) 226 4505.

Third World Network, Africa Secretariat, PO Box 8604, Accra-North, Ghana. Fax: +233 (21) 773857.

Third World Institute (ITeM), Juan Jackson 1136, 11200 Montevideo, Uruguay. Fax: +598 (2) 8 241 9222.

Trans-National Institute, Paulus Potterstraat 20, 1071 DA Amsterdam, The Netherlands. Fax: +31 (20) 673 0179.

UNESCO, 7 place de Fontenoy, 75352 Paris 07 SP, France. Fax: +33 (1) 45 671 690.

UNESCO Publishing, Promotion and Sales Division, 1 rue Miollis, F-75732 Paris Cedex 15, France.

UNRISD, Palais des Nations, 1211 Geneva 10, Switzerland. Fax: +41 (22) 740 0791.

UN University Press, Toho Shimei Building, 15-1 Shibuya 2-chome, Shibuya-ku, Tokyo 150, Japan. Fax: +81 (3) 3406 7345.

Verso, 6 Meard Street, London W1V 3HR, UK. Fax: +4 (171) 734 0059.

Vintage Books, 20 Vauxhall Bridge Road, London SW1X 2SA, UK. Fax: +44 (171) 263 6127.

Zed Books, 7 Cynthia Street, London N1 9JF, UK. Fax: +44 (171) 833 3960.

Development in Practice

Development in Practice is a forum for practitioners, academics, and policy makers to exchange information and analysis concerning the social dimensions of development and emergency relief work. As a multidisciplinary journal of policy and practice, *Development in Practice* reflects a wide range of institutional and cultural backgrounds and a variety of professional experience. *Development in Practice* is published by Oxfam UK & Ireland four times a year; all articles are independently refereed.

Editor Deborah Eade, Oxfam UK & Ireland
Reviews Editor Caroline Knowles, Oxfam UK & Ireland

*Send for a
sample copy now*

*Now also available
on the Internet*

Regular features include:
Main articles
Practical notes
Research round-up
Conference reports
Viewpoint
Feedback
Book reviews

Subscriptions Concessionary rates are available for organisations from developing countries. For a free sample copy and details of subscription rates, please contact:

■ Carfax Publishing Company
   PO Box 25
   Abingdon OX14 3UE
   UK
   fax +44 (0)1235 401551

■ *In North America, contact:*
   Carfax Publishing Company
   875–81 Massachusetts Avenue
   Cambridge MA 02139
   USA
   fax +1 617 354 6875

Development in Practice Readers

A series of thematic selections of papers from past issues of *Development in Practice*. Titles include *Development for Health* (March 1997, introduced by Eleanor Hill) and *Development and Patronage* (September 1997, introduced by Melakou Tegegn). Titles already available are *Development and Social Diversity* (introduced by Mary B Anderson) and *Development in States of War* (introduced by Stephen Commins). Forthcoming titles include *Development and Human Security*.

Oxfam UK & Ireland is registered as a charity no. 202918 and is part of Oxfam International